THE TRAVELING PROFESSOR'S
GUIDE TO PARIS

PROFESSOR STEPHEN C. SOLOSKY

TABLE OF CONTENTS

ABOUT THE AUTHOR

Stephen C. Solosky is a Professor of Mathematics/Statistics/
Information Technology at Nassau Community College, in
Garden City, New York. When he is not traveling, he splits
his time between homes in Garden City, New York and the
Berkshire Mountains of Massachusetts. His favorite place
to visit is Paris, of course. Other international favorites
include Belgium, Spain, England, Germany and Italy. In
the United States, he enjoys spending time in Baltimore,
Annapolis, Chicago, New Orleans, Florida, and Las Vegas.

His guide to Paris has been distributed to thousands of
people worldwide. He is also an engaging and entertaining
speaker. He is widely sought after for his advice on
traveling to Paris and to Europe.

You may contact Professor Solosky at solosks@yahoo.
com or visit his website, http://www.travelingprofessor.
com.

INTRODUCTION

This is my personal guide to Paris. It has been compiled through my many trips to Paris in recent years. Over time, I have made many discoveries and new friends in the City of Light. I have toured virtually every attraction, visited nearly every hotel, and dined at every one of the restaurants listed here. I give my personal recommendations as well as my opinions. In the few instances that I have not personally visited a place mentioned in this guide, the source of that reference is highly reliable.

With this publication I show you some of my favorite spots. I give valuable insight on how to make a vacation to Paris and France enjoyable and enriching. I have included useful time and money-saving tips to let you relish this city without sacrificing luxury or comfort.

This guide is brief and to the point. Not only does it include what just about any traveler to Paris needs to know, it leaves out what you probably don't need to know. I have also included tips and pointers that cannot be found in any other Paris guide book.

One of the great strengths of this book is the scores of useful links. At the click of a mouse, they give up-to-the-minute information on the topics covered here. Almost certainly, there is no other Paris guide book available that can provide the timely data that this book does.

MY FAVORITE MUSEUMS, MONUMENTS, AND ATTRACTIONS

More than any city in the world, Paris is filled with a wide variety of quality attractions. Herein, I have noted the name of the site and the nearest métro station(s). Also noted is the day of the week (if any) the attraction is closed. I follow with a short description then my commentary in italics. Also indicated is if the site accepts the Museum Pass, if applicable, for admission. In short, the Museum Pass is a pay-one-price card that gives unlimited access to over 60 museums and monuments in and near Paris. It is described in greater detail later on.

For most entries, I give a rough estimate of how much time to budget for a visit. Lastly, if there is a useful website associated with the attraction, it has been listed. I urge you to make use of the websites. They give the most up-to-date information on current exhibits, opening times, and special events.

Most museums and monuments have individual admission charges of about 7–10 euros each. In general, churches, cemeteries, public places, and gardens do not have entry fees.

Many museums don't charge an admission fee on the first Sunday of the month. But beware, the crowds can be overwhelming. When visiting museums on a free day, go to the lesser-known places in order to avoid ultra-long lines and overcrowding.

By and large, museums close one day a week, usually Monday or Tuesday. Generally, they also close on May 1, November 11, and December 25. A few museums like the Louvre and the Orsay maintain evening hours one or two days during the week. Some of the smaller museums may close for renovations or the installation of an exhibit. It is best to check the websites of museums to avoid being disappointed.

The listings are in alphabetical order, by keyword. For instance, "Musée de l'Armee" (Army Museum) is listed near the beginning because "Army" is the keyword that people most commonly associate the museum with.

Here are my favorite museums, monuments and attractions:

American Cathedral in Paris
Métro: George V or Alma Marceau
Since 1886, this vibrant and lovely cathedral has served as a center of worship for English speakers in Europe. It is under the direction of the Episcopal Church. Inside, the flag of each state of the United States is flown. *The cathedral maintains an active arts and social program – excellent for those looking to meet other English speakers.* Located at 23, avenue George V. Website: http://www. americancathedral.org

Arc de Triomphe
Métro: Charles De Gaulle – Étoile
Museum Pass: Yes
This is one of the most recognizable monuments in Paris and in the world. France's Unknown Soldier is interred beneath the arch. It is the scene of U.S. soldiers liberating Paris and a symbol of victory for triumphant French troops.

For a challenge, try crossing the street to get to the monument (only kidding!). Actually, there are tunnels under the streets to access the arch. About 40 minutes. Website: http://arc-de-triomphe.monuments-nationaux.fr/en

Stephen C. Solosky

The Cathedral of Notre Dame

Musée de l'Armée (Army Museum)
Métro: Varenne or La Tour Maubourg
Museum Pass: Yes, Closed: 1st Monday of Month (Winter Only)

A museum dedicated to the French military. Military uniforms, weapons, and equipment from all eras of French history dominate this collection. *This is a "do not miss" site. Go to the World War II exhibit and see how De Gaulle won the war. There is a very sobering exhibit in the World War II section on the horrors of the holocaust.* 2 ½ hours. Website: http://www.invalides.org/pages/anglais/menu_ang.html

Musée des Arts et Metiers
Métro: Arts et Metiers
Museum Pass: Yes, Closed: Mondays
This museum contains historical artifacts of engineering, science, and technology. *The first personal computer (so the French claim), the first automobile (so the French claim), and the first airplane (so the French claim) are located here. Foucault's Pendulum, Edison's machines, and TV's from the 1930's make up part of the fascinating collection.* Open late Thursday. 2–3 hours. Website: http://www.arts-et-metiers.net/?lang=ang

Basilique de Saint-Denis (Cathedral Basilica of Saint-Denis)
Métro: Basilique de St-Denis
Museum Pass: Yes
It is the burial place of nearly all the kings and queens of France. *This is one strange place. See the tombs of people you read about in history books – Clovis, Marie Antoinette, Louis XIV. Not for the faint-hearted. I found it fascinating.* 2 hours. 30–40 minute métro ride from center of Paris.
Website: http://saint-denis.monuments-nationaux.fr/en

Place de la Bastille
Métro: Bastille
Much to the surprise and disappointment of many tourists, the infamous Bastille prison is no longer here. *It is the residential neighborhood of hip bars and clubs.*

Bateaux Les Vedettes du Pont-Neuf
Métro: Pont-Neuf
An inexpensive one hour cruise up and down the Seine. Located directly under Pont-Neuf at the tip of Île de la Cité. *This is a good introduction to the city on your first day and a memorable farewell to Paris on your last night there.* Check the website for sailing times and cruise discounts. 1 hour. Website: www.vedettesdupontneuf.com

Bateaux Mouches
Métro: Pont de l'Alma
A trip to Paris is not complete without a cruise down the Seine. It departs across the river from the Eiffel Tower near the Pont de l'Alma. *It is a relaxing and worthwhile tour. I rest my weary legs on the day cruise. In the evening, savor the City of Light in all of its sparkling glory. Also available are lunch and dinner cruises that are enjoyable but pricey.* Website: http://www.bateauxmouches.com

Canal Saint Martin-Canauxrama
Métro: Jaurès
A lovely boat tour through the Canal Saint-Martin. *Take the opportunity to cruise through some of the most adorable neighborhoods in Paris. People watch while you pass through the locks.* Complete with historical commentary. Depart from the Bassin de la Villette and end up at the Bastille. *An easy-going and worthwhile tour. I highly recommend it. Sit at the very front of the boat.* 1 ½ hours. Website: http://www.canauxrama.com/e_saint-martin.htm

Musée Carnavalet
Métro: St-Paul
Museum Pass: Not Required, Closed: Monday
The museum of the history of Paris. The collection here is quite varied. For instance, there are dioramas of the

long-gone Bastille, paintings of the construction of the Statue of Liberty, and personal effects of Marie Antoinette. *Located in the Marais, it is an interesting exhibit.* 1–1 ½ hours. Website: http://www.paris.fr/portail/Culture/Portal.lut?page_id=6468

Catacombs (Les Catacombs)
Métro: Denfert-Rochereau
Museum Pass: No, Closed: Monday
This is an underground quarry that holds about six million skeletons. The Germans used it as bunker and the French Resistance made use of the tunnel system during WW II. *It is absolutely fascinating. Bring a flashlight and watch your head. Some people find it to be great, some find it gruesome. Lots of walking and steps. About 90 minutes.* Website: http://www. catacombes-de-paris.fr/english.htm

Musée National du Moyen Age-Thermes et Hôtel de Cluny (Cluny Museum)
Métro: Cluny La Sorbonne
Museum Pass: Yes, Closed: Tuesday
This museum of medieval art is located in the heart of the Latin Quarter at the intersection of boulevards Saint-Germain and Saint-Michel. It is on the site of ancient Gallo-Roman baths. Contained within are unforgettable works of art from the Middle Ages. *This is one of my favorite hidden gems. The artifacts and famous tapestries are impressive. Have a take-out lunch in the beautiful gardens. Don't miss this one for a relaxing day.* 1 ½ –2 hours. Website: http://www.musee-moyenage.fr/ang

Conciergerie
Métro: Cité
Museum Pass: Yes
This is a former jail that held famous prisoners such as Marie Antoinette and Robespierre during the French

Revolution's Reign of Terror. *Marie Antoinette's jail cell is depicted as it was while she awaited the guillotine. The self-guided tour is interesting, if not a bit cheesy. Movies like "The Three Musketeers" have been filmed inside. It is near Saint-Chapelle and Notre Dame. There is usually a special exhibit at the Conciergerie. 45 minutes.* Website: http://conciergerie. monuments-nationaux.fr/en

Stephen C. Solosky

Rodin's "The Thinker"

La Défense
Métro: La Défense
This is a business area actually located outside the perimeter of Paris at the end of the #1 métro line. The highlight is

the massive, and I mean massive, Grande Arche. Currently the Musée de l'Informatique (History of Computing Museum) is located on the top floor of the Grande Arche. There is a charge to ride the elevator to the top of the arch. *If you have plenty of time and get a kick out of enormous buildings, fit this one in. Since it is a business center, it is dead on the weekends and holidays.* 1 ½ hours. Website: http://www.ladefense.fr/english_english.php

Stephen C. Solosky

Selling candy outside the Pantheon

Eiffel Tower (Tour Eiffel)

Métro: Bir-Hakim or Pont de l'Alma or École Militaire
Museum Pass: No
This is the most recognized landmark in the world. It
was completed in 1889 for the Paris World's Fair. Once
hated by the Parisians, it is now their symbol of pride. *OK,
it's your first trip to Paris. You must visit. Either arrive early in
the morning or later in the evening to avoid the crowds. In my
opinion, it is best viewed from afar at night, especially on one of
the "ponts" crossing the Seine. Watch out for aggressive vendors
and pick-pockets. One hour, unless ascending to the top, which
could take 2–4 hours.* Website: http://www.tour-eiffel.fr/
teiffel/uk

National Museum of Asian Art Guimet

Métro: Iéna
Museum Pass: Yes, Closed: Monday
For those who appreciate Asian art, this museum should
be on the top of the list. The collection is one of the most
impressive outside of Asia. Website: http://www.guimet.
fr/-English-

Musée du Louvre

Métro: Louvre or Palais Royal Musée du Louvre
Museum Pass: Yes, Closed: Tuesday
This is the most acclaimed museum in the world. Its
masterpieces include Mona Lisa, the Code of Hammurabi,
The Crowning of Napoleon, Napoleon's Apartments,
Winged Victory of Samothrace (Nike), Venus de Milo,
Vermeer's "The Lacemaker" and more. The Louvre has an
unparalleled collection of items covering the full spectrum
of art through the ages. The opening and closing scenes
of the motion picture "The Da Vinci Code" were filmed
here. *No doubt an extraordinary museum, but the great pieces
get lost with within its massive space. Go at night – less crowds.*

Only 2–3 hours are needed to visit with careful planning. Check out the marvelous sculptures. Open late on Wednesday and Friday. Museum website: http://www.louvre.fr/llv/commun/home.jsp?bmLocale=en

Luxembourg Gardens
Métro: Odéon or Cardinal Lemoine or Saint-Sulpice
Located in the Latin Quarter. This sizable park is the home to royal gardens and the subject of many Impressionist paintings. *The park is the perfect place for an afternoon stroll. Be like a real Parisian and have a picnic lunch here on a Sunday.*

Musée Marmottan
Métro: Muette
Museum Pass: No, Closed: Monday
A museum containing some fabulous works of Impressionists, especially Monet. *The best kept secret in Paris. A comprehensive collection of Monet's paintings are displayed here in a relaxing atmosphere, quite different from what is found at the Orsay. Impressionist art lovers should not miss this museum. A little bit out of the way. No photos. About 90 minutes to 2 hours.* Website: http://www.marmottan.com/uk

Moulin Rouge
Métro: Blanche
This is the world-famous risqué cabaret house with the 19th century windmill atop of it. It has been entertaining audiences for over a century. *In my opinion, don't waste your time or money on the show. It is a real tourist trap. The Moulin Rouge is in Montmartre. It can be visited during a trip to Sácre-Cœur. Be careful, this is in a safe but seedy area of Paris.* Website: http://www.moulinrouge.fr/home-flash-gb.html

Stephen C. Solosky

Shakespeare & Company is an English Bookstore in Paris

Napoleon's Tomb

Métro: Varenne or La Tour Maubourg
Museum Pass: Yes, Closed: 1st Monday of Month (Winter Only)
The monumental burial place of Napoleon and decorated French military heroes. *Combine with a visit to the Army Museum and Rodin's gardens. It is helpful to have the audio tour.* ½ hour to 45 minutes. Website: http://www.invalides. org/pages/anglais/menu_ang.html

Cathédrale de Notre Dame de Paris (Notre Dame Cathedral)

Métro: Cité or St-Michel Notre Dame
Museum Pass: Only for towers
This cathedral is a classic example of 12th century Gothic architecture. It stands on Île de la Cité and is close to

Sainte-Chapelle and the Conciergerie. *To climb to the top of the cathedral, get there early, before 9 a.m. There is no admission fee to get into the cathedral itself. The Museum Pass does not let you skip the line to climb the towers. Bring binoculars to view the stained glass and other objects. Visit the "Treasury" inside the cathedral. There is a small admission charge. It displays holy relics such as crucifixes and gifts by Popes.* Île Saint-Louis is directly across the bridge from Notre Dame. Sainte-Chapelle and the Conciergerie are also in the immediate area. *This is where I always start my trip in Paris. In the center of the "Parvis" (yes, the spelling is correct) or the plaza in front of the cathedral, notice the bronze marker from which all distances in France are measured.* The Crown of Thorns, worn by Jesus, is put on display at Notre Dame every Friday during Lent and on the 1st Friday of each month. *Watch out for gypsies and pick-pockets. 1–2 hours.* Website: http://www.notredamedeparis.fr

Mary Twiss Connolly

The Basilique du Sacré-Cœur is in Montmartre

Opéra Garnier (Palais Garnier)
Métro: Opéra
Museum Pass: No
A romantic opera house located in the center of the city. Since the construction of the Opéra de Paris Bastille in 1989, the Opéra Garnier is used primarily for ballet performances. *The Opéra is a gorgeous and romantic setting. Many are familiar with it as the home of the "Phantom of the Opera". The Roissybus from CDG drops you here.* Tours in English are held on Wednesday, Saturday, and Sunday at 11:30 and 2:30. From July through August the tours are given every day. 1 hour. Website: http://www.operadeparis.fr

Musée de l'Orangerie
Métro: Concorde
Museum Pass: Yes, Closed: Tuesday
Located in the Tuileries Gardens, near Place de la Concorde. On permanent display are Monet's Nympheas (Water Lilies). Many other works of art from a variety of artists are housed here. The video presentations are excellent. *After many years of renovation, l'Orangerie has re-opened and it is a triumph. It is designed to display Monet's wide paintings and the special exhibits downstairs are enchanting.* Website: http://www.musee-orangerie.fr

Musée d'Orsay
Métro: Solférino
Museum Pass: Yes, Closed: Monday
This grand museum is located in a former railroad station on the left bank. *The building is a work of art in itself. In my opinion, this museum is more enjoyable than the Louvre. Start at the top floor to be treated to the greatest collection of Impressionist paintings in the world. The sculptures are magnificent. Keep an eye out for a few surprises too. Have lunch in the restaurant in the museum. Crowded on*

weekends. I recommend spending two half-days here. Open late Thursday. Website: http://www.musee-orsay.fr/en

Panthéon
Métro: Cardinal Lemoine
Museum Pass: Yes
The resting place of some of Paris' most fêted heroes: Curie, Voltaire, Dumas, Hugo and many more. *It actually took me five trips to Paris before I visited the Panthéon. It is a little bit out of the way from most other attractions. I found it to be quite interesting, primarily because of its massive presence and grandeur. Foucault's Pendulum is on display and a video presentation (in English) is given.* I ¼ hours. Website: http://pantheon.monuments-nationaux.fr/en

Père Lachaise Cemetery (Cimetière du Père-Lachaise)
Métro: Père Lachaise or Philippe Auguste
Museum Pass: No Admission Fee
This is a famous cemetery that is the final resting place of some legendary French and foreign writers, musicians, authors, politicians, and artists. *Jim Morrison, Max Ernst, Maria Callas, Oscar Wilde, Edith Piaf, Gertrude Stein, and many other recognized names are memorialized here. Don't overlook the poignant holocaust monuments. Buy the map at the entrance close to the "Père Lachaise" métro station. Restrooms may not be "modern". Bear in mind that the cemetery is large and may take some time to cover. Wear comfortable shoes, the walkways are cobblestone and the terrain can be hilly.* The website is excellent: http://www.pere-lachaise.com

Musée Picasso
Métro: St-Paul
Museum Pass: Yes, Closed: Tuesday
Located in the Marais, this museum has an engrossing

and varied collection of Picasso works. The museum is located in a 17th century hotel. *This museum is a "must-see" for Picasso fans. Since the works are regularly rotated, I never tire of visiting this museum.* 2 hours. Website: http://www. musee-picasso.fr

Centre Pompidou – Musée National d'Art Moderne
Métro: Rambuteau or Châtelet Les Halles
Museum Pass: Yes, Closed: Tuesday
The Pompidou has an extensive collection of modern (20th century) art. *Despite its popularity, Parisians have mixed feelings regarding this museum. The museum itself is a building that is inside-out. For me, one short visit was enough.* Open until 9 every night. 2 hours. Website: http://www. centrepompidou.fr

Pont-Neuf
Métro: Cité or St-Michel Notre Dame
This bridge (pont) is the oldest in Paris and is depicted in paintings by many celebrated artists. *The bridges over the Seine, especially those near Notre Dame, are most romantic after dark, with a view of the Eiffel Tower in the distance. Generally, these areas are very safe at night.*

Princess Diana (Unofficial) Memorial
Métro: Alma Marceau
Officially, the replica of the torch from the Statue of Liberty at the entrance to the tunnel where Princess Diana lost her life in 1997 stands as a symbol of French-American friendship. Upon her death, people left remembrances and tributes to her at this site. *Whenever I take people to Paris, they consistently ask to see this "memorial" more than any other. Sometimes it is filled with tributes, then there are times when it is nearly barren.* 20 minutes.

Musée Rodin
Métro: Varrene
Museum Pass: Yes, Closed: Monday
This is the former residence of the famous sculptor. It
is surrounded by serene gardens. Now it is the home of
"The Thinker" along with other remarkable sculptures
and works of art. *Enjoy a "croque madame" at the Café du
Musée on the corner. Combine with a trip to Napoleon's Tomb
and the Military Museum.* 1 ½ hours. Website: http://
www.musee-rodin.fr/welcome.htm

Sácre-Cœur
Métro: Abbesses or Anvers
This 19th century basilica was built by on the highest
point in Paris by the French government following the
Franco-Prussian War. It provides a stunning panoramic
view of the city. *Don't walk, but ride the funicular up the hill
to the basilica. Stroll around the lovely neighborhood behind
the church if time permits. Nearby is the Place du Tertre
where many portrait artists will be at work. This is one of the
most popular visitor sites in Paris. Watch for pick-pockets! To
enhance the experience, watch the movie "Amelie" before your
visit.* Website: http://www.sacre-coeur-montmartre.com/us

Sainte-Chapelle
Métro: Cité
Museum Pass: Yes
This is a church dating back to the 13th century. It was
built by King St. Louis to house the Crown of Thorns. It
has the best collection of stained glass of the period. There
are also regularly scheduled concerts here. *This is another
"can't miss" place. Bring a pair of binoculars. Very close to
Notre Dame.* 1 hour. Website: http://sainte-chapelle.
monuments-nationaux.fr/en/?fl_r=4

Mary Twiss Connolly

Crème Brûlée for Dessert in a Paris Bistro

Église Saint-Etienne-du-Mont

Métro: Cardinal Lemoine

Located behind the Panthéon, this Gothic church stands on the site of an abbey founded by Clovis. It is dedicated to St. Genevieve, the patron saint of Paris. *This is a delightful place for a quick rest after visiting the Panthéon. Admire the bright open space of this inviting church before heading onto rue Mouffetard.* ½ hour. Website: http://www.sacred-destinations.com/france/paris-st-etienne-du-mont.htm

Église Saint-Sulpice
Saint-Sulpice

Saint-Sulpice is the setting for a gripping scene in the movie "The Da Vinci Code". Fans of the book and movie are constant visitors. The former prime meridian runs through this church. Catch the renowned organ recitals at the Sunday 10:30 a.m. mass. ½ hour. Website: http://www.stsulpice.com

La Cité des Sciences et de l'Industrie
Métro: Porte de la Villette
Museum Pass: Yes, Closed: Monday

A colossal science museum located on the outskirts of the city. Appropriate for those interested in science and non-scientists alike. *This is another one of the best kept secrets in Paris. It is perhaps the top science museum in the world. I could spend 2 days here – seriously. However, I would say most people visit about half a day. Kids are amazed by this museum, adults are astounded. Many of the exhibits are interactive and can be very contemporary. I understand the Musée de la Musique (website: http://www.cite-musique.fr) is nearby, but I have never been to it. Combine your trip here with a cruise down the Canal St. Martin.* Website: http://www.cite-sciences.fr/english

Musée des Égouts de Paris (Sewers of Paris)
Métro: Pont de l'Alma
Museum Pass: Yes, Closed: Thursday & Friday

This is an hour-long tour of some of the 1,300 miles that make up the Paris sewer system. *I find the tour to be fascinating, others may not be so impressed. It is near the Eiffel Tower, at the Pont de l'Alma. In the hot weather, go here to cool off.* 1 hour. Website (not a good one): http://www.parismuseumpass.com/en/musees_infos_pratiques.php?musee_id=23

Shakespeare & Company

Métro: St-Michel

This is an English bookstore located on the left bank on the Seine across from Notre Dame at 37, rue de la Bûcherie. *It is an interesting place and a great spot to meet other English speakers.* Often open until midnight. Website: http://www.shakespeareco.org

Tuileries Gardens

Métro: Concorde or Tuileries or Palais Royal-Musée du Louvre

The Central Park of Paris, although not as expansive. Located in front of the Louvre on the right bank. *The grounds are perfect for a delightful stroll or a picnic.*

Château de Versailles

Métro: None, take the RERC5

Museum Pass: Yes, Closed: Monday

A stunningly extravagant château and gardens just outside of Paris. It was the palace of the Sun King, Louis XIV and a symbol of the lavish life he led. *Upon seeing the queues here, you'll recognize the value of having the Museum Pass as you go directly to the front of the line. Take the general tour and the special tours. The best way to get to Versailles is to take the RER C5 train which takes about 30 minutes or so. Then, follow the crowd on a 15-minute walk from the station to the château.* ½ to a full day. Website: http://en.chateauversailles.fr

Place du Vert Galant

Métro: Pont-Neuf or Cité

This park is located on the tip of Île de la Cité near Pont-Neuf. *This is a great spot to watch the bateaux go up and down the Seine while enjoying a baguette avec fromage and a taste of wine.*

Place des Vosges

Métro: St-Paul

Located in the heart of the Marais, this is the oldest public square in Paris. It is surrounded by picturesque 17th century townhouses. *Drop in on the splendid art galleries around the square. Visit Victor Hugo's home at 6, place de Vosges.* 30–45 minutes. Victor Hugo home website: http://www.hugo-online.org/Paris/maison.html

PARIS MUSEUM PASS

You must buy the Museum Pass (MP). It comes in 2, 4, and 6 consecutive day options for 32, 48 and 64 euros respectively. The primary advantage to the MP is that the regular admission lines can be skipped to gain entrance into most of the museums and monuments. It's a money-saver too. Buy it any place that accepts the Museum Pass. However, it is best to purchase it where there are fewer crowds (Cluny, Conciergerie, etc.) to avoid waiting in line. It can also be purchased at the orange Tourisme Information booths at the airport and at FNAC stores located throughout Paris. Travelers under age 18 do not need a MP if they are accompanying an adult. Website: http://www.parismuseumpass.com/en

NEIGHBORHOODS

Each Parisian neighborhood has its own distinctive personality. Some are chic, some are smutty. Some are sophisticated, some are cultured, and others are crude. They all have an element of "*je ne sais quoi*" that makes each one of them appealing in their own way.

Here are my picks for the best neighborhoods to visit:

Rue Cler
Métro: École Militaire
This energetic cobblestone street has lively restaurants, cafés, and shops near the Eiffel Tower. A very Parisian type of neighborhood street. Many Americans like this area to stay, dine, and relax in. A market is there on Sundays.

Montmartre
Métro: Abesses or Anvers
This is the most frequently visited tourist area in Paris. It is in a hilly and rural neighborhood near the outskirts of the city. It has charming homes, shops, cafés, and bistros. This area is not known for quality hotels. Take the métro to the Abbesses station to start the visit. Sácre-Cœur is here as well as Moulin Rouge and Place du Tertre. Parts of Montmartre can be sketchy at night – especially Place Pigalle. Watch out for gypsies and pick pockets. ½ to ¾ of a day if you go to Sácre-Cœur, Place du Tertre, and the surrounding neighborhood.

Champs-Élysées
Métro: Charles de Gaulle – Étoile or Franklin D. Roosevelt or Champs-Élysées Clemenceau
The Times Square of Paris. It extends from the Place de

Concorde (at the end of the Tuileries) to the Place de l'Étoile (where the Arc de Triomphe is located). It is the scene of wild celebrations following sporting victories, national accomplishments, and special events. Glitzy stores, cinemas, and galleries line the street. I don't particularly like this neighborhood, but some are impressed by its aura.

Latin Quarter
Métro: St-Michel, Cardinal Lemoine, Cluny-La Sorbonne, Place Monge and more
The area on the left bank that has traditionally been the home of students, classic cafés, and a lively village-like atmosphere. It is a great walking neighborhood. I would compare it to the East Village in New York City. This is my most favorite place to stay.

Île Saint-Louis
Métro: No métro station on Île Saint-Louis. Cité is closest
This is a traditional Parisian neighborhood of cobblestone streets, cafés, bistros, pâtisseries, boulangeries and quaint shops. It is just over the bridge from Notre Dame and Île de la Cité. Some charming small hotels and B&B's are located here. Get a true flavor of Paris while walking through this neighborhood. Cross the bridge (often there are street performers here) from Notre Dame to get there. Have ice cream at Berthillon's. Afterwards, take a stroll down the Seine towards the Eiffel Tower.

Marais
Métro: St-Paul
This is the Jewish and the gay section of Paris. It is a revitalized neighborhood that has regained prominence in the arts and culture and in dining. It is a charming walking neighborhood. Eat a falafel at L'as du Fallafel on rue des Rosiers and have a pain au chocolate from one

of the bakeries. The Picasso Museum, Place des Vosges, and Carnavalet (history of Paris museum) are in the neighborhood. 3 hours. A full day if you visit the museums.

Saint Germain des-Prés
Métro: St Germain des-Prés
Adjacent to the Latin Quarter on the left bank. It is the home of chic shops, time-honored restaurants, good shopping, and trendy art galleries. There are many good, moderately priced hotels in this area. It lacks the glitz of Champs-Élysées but it is more of a traditional French neighborhood. If you want an area to comfortably walk to a mix of restaurants, shops, cultural locales, markets, gardens, and theaters – Saint Germain des-Prés is for you.

Bercy
Métro: Cour St-Émilion
Once I was in Paris, and due to the international air show, not a bed was to be had near the center of town.
I reluctantly took a room in the outskirts of Paris in Bercy.
I was pleasantly surprised. Nearby Bercy Village has a nice collection of shops, bars, and restaurants. The Cour St-Émilion métro station is on what is called the "meteor" métro line. It provides speedy access into the center of Paris. Bercy wouldn't be my first choice as a place to stay, but I certainly would not be unhappy being there.

Mouffetard
Métro: Place Monge
Rue Mouffetard is an old Parisian neighborhood full of charm. Located in the Latin Quarter, behind the Panthéon, this is an eclectic area of boutiques, inexpensive ethnic restaurants, and a typical Parisian market. Some claim it is too touristy, others love it. Either way, it is certainly worth a visit.

Stephen C. Solosky

The heart of the Latin Quarter

FAVORITE DINING SPOTS FOR EVERY TASTE AND BUDGET

Parisians have dinner later in the evening than we do, but most restaurants are open for dinner at 6 or 7 p.m. Dress is a little bit more formal (no jeans or sneakers) than in the U.S. It is easy to spend $1,000 for dinner at places like l'Ambroise, Alain Ducasse at the Hôtel Plaza Athénée, or Le Grand Véfour. Then again, there are plenty of good places for fewer than 100 euros or even 50 euros (with wine) for two. I think someone can even get away with spending under 20 euros for a decent meal by steering clear of the tourist areas.

At top restaurants, reservations are a must. If there is a place in mind where you want to dine, make reservations through your hotel concierge, by phone, or just stop by the restaurant a few days in advance. It's often possible to request a reservation by e-mail, but be certain to get a reservation confirmation. See the notes I have made regarding reservations on some of my selections.

By law, all restaurants must display their menus with prices outside the restaurant. In almost all cases, the price includes tax and tip. See the section on "Tipping" later on in this guide.

I need to say that half the fun of dining in Paris is finding and discovering favorite restaurants on your own, but here are my picks, listed by arrondissement:

L'Ardoise, 28, rue du Mont-Thabor, 1st arrondissement. Métro: Concorde or Tuileries.
I have eaten at this bistro a few times and it is always good.

It is popular with locals as well as tourists. Inventive French offerings are ordered from a blackboard menu. The seating can be tight and there may be a wait for a table. Reserve a day or two in advance.

Angelina, 226, rue de Rivoli, 1st arrondissement.
Métro: Concorde or Tuileries.
This is a world-famous salon de thé on Rue de Rivoli near the Louvre along the Tuileries Gardens. This is a touristy place that reputedly serves the best hot chocolate in Paris accompanied by divine pastries.

Brasserie du Louvre, Located in the Hôtel du Louvre, Place Andre Malraux, 1st arrondissement.
Métro: Palais Royal or Musée du Louvre.
This smart-looking restaurant is in the shadow of the great museum on rue de Rivoli. It is nothing special, I just like it. Reservations not necessary. About 125 euros for two.
Website: http://www.hoteldulouvre.com

Aux Lyonnais, 32, rue St-Marc, 2nd arrondissement.
Métro: Bourse or Richelieu-Drouot.
An Alain Ducasse restaurant for 100 euros for two? You bet. One of my faves. Lyonnais cuisine is known for its hearty dishes of pork, veal, tripe, and poached fish. Reserve a day or two ahead of time. Website: http://www.alain-ducasse.com/public_us/cest_aussi/fr_aulyonnais.htm

Chez Jenny, 39, rue du Temple, 3rd arrondissement.
Métro: République.
A big, bright, lively Alsatian spot near the Place de la République. Alsatian restaurants generally have hearty dishes. I like the traditional choucroute garnie dish with a bottle of gewurztraminer. Those not conversant in French might have some difficulty. Reservations needed

for weekends. Moderate (100 euros for two). Website: http://www.chez-jenny.com/en

Bofinger, 5, rue de la Bastille, 4th arrondissement. Métro: Bastille.
A turn-of-the-century Parisian favorite with an Alsatian bias. The shellfish platter is the superstar here. Even though the crowd is mostly French, I found the management and waiters to be quite friendly and accommodating. It is moderately priced. It's near the Bastille opera house, so it's difficult to get a table immediately before or after the opera. Reserve a day or two in advance. Website: http://www.bofingerparis.com/en

L'As du Fallafel, 34, rue des Rosiers, 4th arrondissement. Métro: St-Paul.
This Jewish deli-type restaurant in the Marais is a real crowd-pleaser. I like it so much for their 5–7 euro falafels (they call them "Cocktail de Viandes" which literally means "Meat Cocktail) that I keep their business card tacked on my corkboard in my kitchen. A great little take-away ("emporter" in French) place or fine for a sit-down lunch. I highly recommend this restaurant.

Berthillon, 29-31, rue Saint Louis en l'ile, 4th arrondissement. Métro: Cité.
This well-known ice cream shop and salon de thé is located on Île Saint-Louis. The ice cream flavors are heavenly, especially the fruit flavors. Some say they have the best ice cream in the world – try the pampelmousse. They are closed in August – yes that's right – closed in August. Website: http://www.berthillon.fr

Café Le Petit Pont, 1, rue du Petit Pont, 5th arrondissement. Métro: St-Michel.

What a view of Notre Dame from the left bank! I have spent many a late evening sitting at this café with friends. Sometimes they have jazz or a piano player in the evenings. The location and ambience is what makes this place special – not the food. It is very close to Shakespeare & Company bookstore (see entry under "My Favorite Museums, Monuments, and Attractions").

Le Pré Verre, 8, rue Thenard, 5th arrondissement. Métro: Maubert-Mutualite.
You know it has to be good if the Parisians line up to get into the place. It is near the Cluny, across the street from the Hôtel du College de France. The French food here is complemented with spices, especially those of the Asian variety. They offer a prix fixe menu for about 30 euros that makes it the best dinner bargain in Paris. The lunch formule costs half of that. Make a reservation a day or two beforehand for the upstairs room. I enthusiastically recommend this restaurant. Website: http://www.lepreverre.com

Le Coupe Chou, 9-11, rue de Lanneau, 5th arrondissement. Métro: Maubert-Mutualite.
Americans seem to love this place located in the Latin Quarter. The fireplace and candlelit setting make it a favorite for romantics. The French food is better than average and moderately priced. Reservations are not usually required. Website: http://www.lecoupechou.com/English-informations_r28.html

Brasserie Lipp, 151, boulevard Saint Germain, 6th arrondissement.
Métro: St Germain des-Prés.
I had my first meal ever in Paris here. The menu is traditional French/Alsatian. The menu (except for

the prices) has not changed in 75 years. Try Chartier for something on the same style, but less expensive Reservations a day or two before dining are recommended. Ask to be seated on the main floor. Dinner for two is about 125–150 euros or so. Website: http://www.ila-chateau.com/lipp

Les Éditeurs, 4, Carrefour de l'Odéon, 6th arrondissement. Métro: Odéon.
I never had dinner here but I would rendezvous with my French friends for a café au lait or a light snack. Look closely, you might spot a celebrity here. Inexpensive. Website: http://www.lesediteurs.fr

Bistrot d'Henri, 16, rue Princesse, 6th arrondissement. Métro: St Germain des-Prés or Saint-Sulpice.
This is a well-liked and friendly spot. The tables are close, but that's fine because everyone always seems to be social and willing to share their travel tales. The food is good. My lunch (for 2) cost 54 euros with wine.

Pâtisserie Viennoise, 8, rue de l'École de Médecine, 6th arrondissement.
Métro: Odéon.
What a classic pastry shop! I go out of my way to have breakfast here. Sit down inside with the Sorbonne students if you wish. Angelina may have the reputation of having the best hot chocolate in town, but Pâtisserie Viennoise's is better. Closed weekends.

Les Bouquinistes, 53, Quai des Grands Augustins, 6th arrondissement.
Métro: St-Michel.
This left-bank Guy Savoy restaurant is in the shadow of the Notre Dame Cathedral. It is good, trendy, and hip. I thought

this restaurant was the perfect choice for a Valentine's Day dinner I recently enjoyed here. About 200 euros for two. Website: http://www.lesbouquinistes.com/en

A La Petite Chaise, 36 rue de Grenelle, 7th arrondissement.
Métro: Rue du Bac.
This (not le Procope) is the oldest restaurant in Paris.
It is cozy, charming, and classic. It is authentically French.
I found the staff to be obliging and the food to be good.
The prix fixe menu is a good value. Website: http://www.
alapetitechaise.fr/english.htm

Café Constant, 139, rue St. Dominique, 7th arrondissement.
Métro: École Militaire.
Casual. Great French food at reasonable prices. Get
the "Île Flotante" for dessert. One of my top picks.
Near Champ de Mars and Rue Cler. 110 euros for two.
Website: http://www.cafeconstant.com

Les Cocottes, 135, rue St. Dominique. 7th arrondissement.
Métro: École Militaire.
Another Christian Constant gem. Set up almost like an
American diner, it is casual and not expensive. The unique
main dishes are served *en cocotte*, or casserole style. You
are most likely to see Chef Constant there, and most likely,
he would love to chat with you.

Chartier, 7, rue Faubourg Montmartre, 9th arrondissement.
Métro: Grands Boulevards.
I eat here at least once <u>every</u> time I go to Paris. It's
common to find yourself sharing a water bottle and bread
basket with a Parisian or someone from Finland, Warsaw,
Buenos Aires, or Seoul. The food is not the best, but go
here to eat as the Parisians have been doing for over a
century. It's a lot of fun. Get an appetizer (called an entrée

in Paris), a plat (what we call an entrée in the U.S., dessert, wine (or water) for about 20 euros. No reservations, just line up outside and chat up the friendly crowd while waiting to be seated. They stop seating at precisely 10 p.m. Website: http://www.restaurant-chartier.com

Stephen C. Solosky
Standing Guard Atop the Cathedral of Notre Dame

Chez Michel, 10, rue de Belzunce, 10th arrondissement. Métro: Gare du Nord or Poissonnière.

Don't expect to find many tourists at this small restaurant serving Breton-style dishes of the French seacoast. The place is hard to find, but your taste buds will be rewarded for the effort. It should be less than 100 euros for two, with wine. I would reserve a day or two in advance, although I walked in with no problem. Ask to be seated on the main floor for a more intimate experience, downstairs for a communal environment. No air conditioning. Chez Michel is one of my top choices.

Le Train Bleu, Located in the Gare de Lyon train station in the 12th arrondissement. The beauty and grandeur of this Belle Époque restaurant more than compensates for the mediocre food. In all fairness, I was with a group of about 20 people and we ordered from a special menu. Cocktails were an exorbitant 14 euros each. As I said, the food was unexceptional, but everyone else I know of who has eaten here likes it. It is expensive and reservations are recommended. No air conditioning. Website: http://www.le-train-bleu.com/uk/navigation.htm

Le Beurre Noisette, 68, rue Vasco de Gama, 15th arrondissement.
Métro: Lourmel or Porte de Versailles.
It is hard to get to and there won't be many tourists there either. Chef Thierry Blanqui, formerly of the long-established La Tour d'Argent reinvents traditional French cuisine.
Service is casual, but the food is good. If you are in the area, it is the place to be. About 100 euros for two.

Other Recommendations:

- For a very romantic dinner, try 1728 in the 8th (8 rue d'Anjou, Métro: Concorde or Madeleine).

Website: http://www.restaurant-1728.com. I can't remember dining at a more amorous setting. It is less expensive than comparable restaurants.

- **Léon de Bruxelles** is a chain of inexpensive to moderate brasseries. I like it for a quick and simple meal of moules frites (mussels and fries) and other Belgian treats. Website (French only): http://www. leon-de-bruxelles.fr
- For a variety of inexpensive restaurants with good food and service, go to rue Grégoire de Tours between rue de Buci and Boulevard St. Germain near the Odéon métro station in the 6th,.
My favorite is **Au Beaujolais** at 9, rue Grégoire de Tours. Be sure to tell Hakim that I sent you!
- Rue Mouffetard in the Latin Quarter (métro Place Monge or Censier Daubenton) has an assortment of ethnic restaurants offering meals at popular prices. For a little more money, go over to rue Cler (métro École Militaire) with all of the other Americans to enjoy a good meal.

Also, take a look in the New York Times online edition (www.nytimes.com). Go to the Paris Destination Guide in the travel section and search for an article "Does the Affordable Paris Bistro Still Exist? Oui" by Mark Bittman. There are some excellent reviews of inexpensive Paris bistros. I have eaten in nearly all of them.

A word of warning: rue de la Huchette. This is a pedestrian street located in the Latin Quarter starting at boulevard Saint-Michel (métro: St-Michel). It is full of souvenir shops and lively, inexpensive falafel shops and restaurants (mostly Greek and Asian). There have been reports of unclean conditions and some cases of food poisoning. I personally never have had a problem here. However, I urge caution.

When dining, address your server as "monsieur" or "madame". In general, the bill may not be brought to the table unless requested as in "Monsieur, l'addition, s'il vous plâit?"

Finally, many restaurants propose a "prix fixe" meal called a "formule" (usually for lunch) or a "menu" for dinner. In essence, it is an entrée, plat, dessert, and sometimes wine and coffee for a set price. In my judgment, this is usually a good, if not the best value.

WINE BARS

There are few experiences more Parisian than spending an afternoon at a "Bar à Vins". Wine bars are casual places for people to meet, enjoy some light fare (how about a dozen oysters and a plate of saucissons and fromage?), and drink wine.

Here are some of my favorite wine bars in Paris:

Bistrot Melac, 42 rue Léon Frot, 11ᵗʰ.
Métro: Charonne
Since 1938 people have been discovering little-know wines from the Languedoc and Loire regions here. The menu features foods from the Aveyron region, famous for its cheeses. Website: http://www.melac.fr/pages/english.html

Stephen C. Solosky
The Royal Château of Versailles is the Former Home of Marie Antoinette

Racines, Passage des Panoramas, 2nd.
Métro: Grands Boulevards
Located in an enclosed passageway, this relatively new wine bar features organic wines. Open weekdays. Website: http://www.paris-update.com/restaurants/racines.htm

L'Ecluse, 15, quai des Grands Augustins, 6th.
Métro: St-Michel
This wine bar offers delectable wines with simple, seasonal cuisine. They boast that over 600,000 glasses of Bordeaux are served annually here. There are also four other locations. Website: http://www.leclusebaravin.com/us

Le Baron Bouge, 1, rue Théophile Roussel, 12th.
Métro: Ledru-Rollin
This is what comes to mind when you think "Bar à Vins". It is filled with market traders and flea market shoppers during the day. At night, the young, hip crowd comes alive.

Stephen C. Solosky

A Flower in Bloom in Monet's Garden in Giverney

Taverne Henri IV, 13 place du Pont-Neuf, 1st.
Métro: Cité or Pont-Neuf
Conveniently located near the most popular tourist sites on the tip of Île de la Cité, it is a quiet spot for some good wines and relaxation.

CONCERTS

I love to attend classical music concerts while in Paris. The schedule for concerts held at Sainte-Chapelle, the American Cathedral in Paris can be found at http://www. ampconcerts.com.

Another venue is Église Saint-Sulpice which hosts organ concerts at the Sunday 10:30 a.m. mass that are quite grand. The metro station is Saint-Sulpice. Website: http:// stsulpice.com/Docs/concerts.html

Another good guide for finding all types of concerts is this website: http://www.fnacspectacles.com

The FNAC site is mostly in French, but easy enough to figure out. There are several FNAC department stores located throughout Paris. They sell tickets for all types of concerts and performances. From there, browse and buy tickets for virtually any performance in Paris.

Paris has two major opera houses. They host a variety of performances in addition to opera, especially at the Palais (Opéra) Garnier. The website is: http://www. operadeparis.fr/cns11/live/onp/site/index.php?lang=en

If staying in a business class hotel, the concierge may assist you in acquiring tickets.

SMOKING

I used to say that Parisian restaurants have two sections: smoking and chain-smoking. Happily for most, this is no longer the case. Although laws have been passed in an effort to ban smoking in restaurants, a few people still do it. In some of the hotel rooms I have stayed in, I have detected a slight cigarette smoke odor. Keep this in mind when booking a room.

Stephen C. Solosky

The Picasso Museum is in the Marais

FLEA MARKETS

There are quite a few flea markets all over Paris. Bring cash and be prepared to haggle for the best price. However, items at Paris flea markets are rarely bargains. Watch for pick-pockets and scam artists.

Here are two of my favorite flea markets:

Les Puces de Paris
Métro: Porte de Clignancourt or Porte de St-Ouen.
This is the mother of all flea markets. It might just be the largest in the world. Open Saturday through Monday from 7:30 a.m. to 6 p.m. It is enormous, but savvy flea market shoppers go to the smaller market at Porte de Vanves.
Website: http://www.parispuces.com

Marché aux Puces de la Porte de Vanves
Located on avenue Georges Lafenestre & avenue Marc Sangnier.
Métro: Porte de Vanves.
This is a smaller flea market but the vendors at les Puces de Paris can often be found here buying merchandise for their larger market. Open weekend mornings.

STREET MARKETS

One of the great pleasures of visiting Paris is in strolling through the amiable street markets scattered throughout the city. Having such tempting produce, cheese, meats, breads, and other delectable items at your fingertips makes you want consider cancelling your flight home and just staying here forever.

I suggest visiting these street markets:

Marché Raspail. Rue Cherche Midi/Rue de Rennes in the 6th. Rennes or Babylone métro station. An organic food market on Sunday morning and on Tuesday. On Friday it offers a wider variety of products.

Marché Montorgeuil. Rue Montorgeuil in the 2nd. Located near the Les Halles métro. This is a charming street market from the good old days. Open Tuesday and Sunday.

Marché Mouffetard. Some people like this enchanting market best of all. It is crowded with cafés and bars. Some people think marché Mouffetard is everything Paris should be. Merchants offer local products and items from all over the world. Even when the market is not open it is busy with interesting boutiques, restaurants, and shops. The market is Tuesday through Sunday. Métro: Place Monge or Censier-Daubenton.

Marché Rue de Buci. There is more than one excuse to visit this compact market in Saint Germain des-Prés.

Not only are there the traditional vendors but cafés, pâtisseries, salon de thés, bookstores, and a wide variety of shops and boutiques are found here. Open daily. Located near the Odéon or Mabillon métro.

Stephen C. Solosky

A Poissonnier at the Rue Buci Marketplace

SHOPPING

This is one area where I have little expertise. I rarely shop while I am in Paris. However, Paris does have some large department stores (les Grands Magasins). The Champs-Élysées is a popular shopping spot to find contemporary chic fashions.

Along boulevard Hausmann in the Opéra district there are the more traditional department stores like Au Printemps and Galleries Lafayette. From November through December, check out the jolly holiday window displays. Other popular shopping locations include le Bon Marché on the left bank, and BHV which is a combination of a French Home Depot and Macy's rolled into one.

Here are some links to investigate:
http://www.discoverfrance.net/France/Paris/Shopping/Paris_deptstores.shtml and
http://www.10best.com/Paris/Shopping/Department_Stores/index.html.

ARE PARISIANS RUDE?

French etiquette dictates that a greeting is to be extended before a conversation is initiated. I usually say "bonjour, hello" to show my appreciation for their language but that I speak English. I rarely have an issue with Parisians if I follow their protocol. After all, I am in their country. If I don't follow their rules, they may feel that I am the one being rude.

It is true that some Parisian waiters can be surly. But that's part of the reason why Paris is so much fun! Seriously, if you encounter a rude waiter, be polite but firm. Generally, they will back right down and quickly become your best friend.

All in all, I need to emphasize that the overwhelming majority of Parisians are friendly, gracious, and hospitable.

TIPPING

In nearly all restaurants, the tip is included in the price of the meal. The menu will indicate this by stating "service compris". Americans sometimes feel uncomfortable about leaving no tip or a small tip. In a moderately priced restaurant, a two euro tip per person is generous. Trust me, anything more is excessive.

If using a concierge service at a business-class hotel, it is a good idea to leave a tip. If I find the concierge being helpful, I will give a 10–20 euro tip at the beginning of my stay and another 10–20 at the end.

At a bar, a one or two euro tip after the bill is received is very generous. The same principle applies for a taxi ride.

Stephen C. Solosky
Nearly All Restaurants Display Their Menus Outside

LANGUAGE AND CUSTOMS

Is it necessary to speak French to get by? Absolutely not. In fact, in the tourist areas of Paris, you might hear English spoken more than on the streets of Manhattan. A good percentage of Parisians understand basic English and many signs are also in English. However, make an effort to use the French you already know as in "bonjour", "merci", "s'il vous plâit", and "pardon".

One thing you may have trouble with if you don't know ANY French is reading a menu. It wouldn't be a bad idea to get a basic French language book describing what might be found on a menu rather than using the risky "point and pray" method when ordering.

The French tend to be a bit more formal than we are here in the United States. As mentioned before, I always greet any Parisian, including retail clerks, civil service workers, or anyone else for that matter, with "bonjour, hello" before I begin a conversation. Each time, I end my exchange with "merci" or "au revoir". I always offer a lady my seat on a crowded bus or métro.

VAT – THE INSIDE SCOOP

The VAT (Value Added Tax) is like a hidden sales tax (about 19.6%) added on to just about everything you buy. For large purchases (over 175 euros) on items like jewelry, clothes, or works of art, ask the retailer how to get the VAT refunded. Here is a website for more info: http://www.globalrefund.com

Mary Twiss Connolly

The Treats of a Boulangerie are Nothing Short of Divine

HANDICAPPED ACCESS

Unfortunately Paris and Europe in general, does not provide the services and accommodations for the handicapped or elderly that we have here in the U.S. Please be aware that some buildings and public transportation have inadequate facilities for those who may be physically challenged. Furthermore, some streets are paved in cobblestone making walking on them difficult without appropriate footwear. A few restaurants and facilities still have Turkish toilets. And, for those who don't know what a Turkish toilet is, see this: http://www. hurktoilet.nl/hurk-en.php

MONEY MATTERS

In France and in much of Europe, the euro is the standard currency. U.S. dollars are not accepted. If possible, bring some euros along when departing for Paris. However, it is not absolutely necessary.

Try to avoid using currency exchange offices to change dollars into euros. The commissions can be excessive.

In Paris, I advise using credit cards as much as possible to get the true conversion rate. However, most banks assess a foreign transaction fee (about 3%) when making charges. The exception is the Capital One credit card. There are no such fees.

Foreign transaction fees apply when using an ATM. Once again, the exception is the Capital One bank card. There are plenty of ATM's in Paris and an American-issued bank card will work with them. To be on the safe side, bring at least 2 different ATM cards along with at least one of them being from a major U.S. bank like Citibank or Chase. I had trouble getting money with an ATM card from my local credit union. Since about 2002, the dollar has weakened significantly against the euro. In July of 2009, it costs about $1.40 to get a euro. For the latest exchange rate, check out: http://finance.yahoo.com/currency/convert?amt=1&from=EUR&to=USD&submit=Convert

Before I depart for my trip, I notify my bank that I will be traveling to Europe and using my credit or bank card on the trip.

At train stations there are kiosks where tickets may be purchased. Usually, American credit cards do not work here as they do not have a certain microchip embedded in them that the European cards have.

TRANSPORTATION – GET TO AND FROM EVERYWHERE WITHIN PARIS

If you ask me, you have to be out of your mind to be a tourist and drive a car in Paris. The traffic is awful, the roads are unfamiliar, and parking is a nightmare. Gas costs much more than it does in the U.S. The public transportation system is so good, there is no need to drive. When taking a side trip outside of Paris, take a train to your first destination then rent a car from there. For instance, when I went to the Loire Valley, I took the train to Tours and rented my car there.

The Paris métro system is one of the best in the world. It is safe, clean, efficient, designed well, and it runs frequently. Rarely is there more than a 5–10 minute walk to get to a métro station. The métro system stops running at about 12:30 a.m. on weekdays and about 1:30 a.m. on weekends. It commences at about 5:30 a.m. every day.

The bus system is good too. The same tickets are used for both the bus and métro system. Buy individual tickets at about 1.60 euro per ticket, or a "carnet" of 10 tickets for about 11.60 euros. A métro or bus ride costs the same, regardless of distance traveled within the city. Another option is to purchase the "Passe Navigo Découverte" commuter pass for about 16 euros a week plus a 5 euro fee to get the initial Passe Navigo Découverte. It gives unlimited access to the métro and bus system for a week, but it only starts on a Monday. A small photo (a reduced in size copy of your passport photo will suffice) is required to obtain and use the pass.

Note that as of April 1, 2010, the weekly transportation pass will be known as the Navigo Semaine.

When using a ticket to travel, make sure to hold onto it until exiting the bus, métro, or train station. Although it is uncommon, inspectors can assess a fine on the spot to those not holding a ticket.

Don't get persuaded into buying the Paris Visite pass. It is rarely an advantage to do so.

For métro/bus/RER maps, go to: http://www.ratp.fr

Stephen C. Solosky

An Entrance to a Métro Station in Montmartre

TOURING PARIS BY BIKE OR BUS

I am not a big fan of organized tours. It is my general philosophy that a traveler explores and discovers on his own, whereas a tourist is limited to only what is shown to him. However, there are times when an organized touring activity is fun and worthwhile.

Here are my two recommendations:

Fat Tire Bike Tours
I love the FTBT. Biking around Paris is fun and a good opportunity to meet other travelers. It's also a way to get some exercise. The tour is organized with a maximum of 20 bikers meeting at the Eiffel Tower. The day tour cycles by landmarks like Napoleon's Tomb, the Louvre, and the Orsay. A lunch break at the Tuileries presents the opportunity to relax and make new friends. On the evening tour, see the sites while pedaling over to Île Saint-Louis. Then, leave the bikes behind for a starlit cruise down the Seine with a glass of French wine in hand. Website: http://fattirebiketours.com/paris

Hop-On, Hop-Off (HOHO) Bus
If feeling a bit lazy and you want to leave the driving to someone else, try a HOHO open bus tour. You will get a better feel of the layout of the city as opposed to traveling underground. There are a couple of open bus tours but the one I like is the Paris l'Open Tour. The cost is 29 euros for one day, 32 euros for 2 days (hint: get the 2-day pass). Children cost 15 euros for two days. Website: http://www.pariscityrama.com/paris-open-tour

WHAT YOU CAN'T GET IN PARIS

Paris is a big city. There are supermarkets, drugstores, convenience stores, etc. In short, they have everything in Paris that we have here in the U.S., except on a smaller scale. Until the arrival Starbucks, the only thing you couldn't get in Paris that you could get in the U.S. was coffee in a paper cup!

Sundry items like film, detergent, deodorant, and shaving cream can be expensive in Paris. Consider carrying them along from the U.S.

WHAT TO WEAR

To look like a tourist, wear sneakers, shorts, t-shirt and anything with a logo on it. To blend in and look like a Parisian, wear long pants (jeans are OK), dark shirt, and comfortable shoes. And to really fit in, a nice scarf will do it. I know I am assimilating myself to the French culture when the French come up to me to ask me questions.

Stephen C. Solosky
A Stylish Scarf is the Perfect Fashion Accessory for Anyone Visiting Paris

WHEN TO VISIT

In the summer, the airfares are expensive, the hotels charge "peak" prices, the city is crowded and the weather can be hot. And remember, A/C is not as prevalent in Paris as it is in the U.S. Furthermore, many of the best restaurants and a good number of shops are closed in August while many Parisians go on holiday. I like traveling during the off-peak period which is from the middle of October until the middle of May.

Be wary of traveling when special events like the Paris air show is going on (usually in June, every other year) or during sporting events like major soccer tournaments. It can be brutally crowded and expensive at these times.

WEATHER

The inconsistent Paris weather never ceases to amaze me.
In January it can snow, but rarely more than an inch or two.
The weather can be cold in the winter (35–45 degrees).
Yet, I recall it being 70 degrees one day in February. It
usually rains like cats and dogs in the springtime. In fact,
it rains about 165 days per year. Once I was there in late
June and it was in the 50's. Sometimes in the summer it
can get into the 90's. Regardless of season, I always bring
an umbrella. A light jacket in the summer months might be
a good idea. The fall is usually mild.

For Paris weather, check this link:
http://www.weather.com/outlook/travel/businesstraveler/
local/FRXX0076?from=search_city

Stephen C. Solosky

The Bouquinistes Can be Found Along the Seine Selling Their Ancient
Books

PACKING LIST

I recommend packing as lightly as possible. I go on 14-day European trips with just a carry-on luggage. Paris does not have as many elevators or escalators as there are in the U.S. Don't be inconvenienced by dragging cumbersome bags up and down stairs or trying to cram bulky luggage into small taxis. As for clean clothes, I do hand laundry in my hotel room or I find a full-service laundromat to drop off clothes for pick up later in the day.

Here are some items that I bring on every trip:

- **Comfortable Walking Shoes** – this is my #1 recommendation. Not only is there a lot of walking in Paris, but there are plenty of stairs and some hilly areas. On a few occasions, there is walking on uneven surfaces such as cobblestone. Bring band-aids for those blisters, too.
- **Umbrella** – it rains quite regularly, especially in the springtime.
- **Binoculars** – great for close up looks at all of that stained glass.
- **Passport** – bring at least 2 color passport copies in addition to your original. In case of a lost passport, it is much easier to replace if you have a copy. Sometimes hotels ask to leave a copy of your passport with them. In that situation, just give them a photocopy. Lastly, some transportation options such as the "Passe Navigo Découverte" require a photo. Just reduce the size of the passport photo by about 40% when you photocopy it. Then, snip the photo from the photocopy and apply it to your métro pass.

- **Two ATM Cards** – preferably from a major bank. Make sure there is money in the checking account.
- **30–50 Euros** – just to get started before hitting an ATM.
- **Electric Plug Adapter** – to charge a cell phone, camera, etc., a 2 pin 220 volt adapter is needed. In Paris it can be found at BHV (a department store near the Hôtel de Ville) or the Au Vieux Campeur, a camping store with multiple locations in the Latin Quarter. In the U.S., pick one up at Radio Shack.
- **Métro/Bus/RER Map** – available at http://www. ratp.info/informer/anglais/index.php#
- **Student/Teacher/Senior Citizen ID** – numerous discounts are available for those fitting into any of these categories.
- **Driver's License** – More and more places like hotels, restaurants, and shops want to see some type of official picture ID when you use a credit card. Your local driver's license will do the trick.
- **Plastic Shopping Bags** – supermarkets can charge a fee for plastic shopping bags. Bring some from home if planning to shop for groceries. Plastic bags also have other uses beyond the supermarket.

MEETING PEOPLE AND MAKING NEW FRIENDS

Most of the time, I travel alone to Paris. I love the freedom to walk wherever I want to go and at my own pace. I can discover more, and spend as much time as I like when I go solo. There are times, however, when I do want to socialize and meet up with others.

The websites www.traveldaddy.com, www.meetup.com and www.virtualtourist.com have listings of "meetings" where travelers can connect with each other. This usually involves having dinner or some other type of similar activity with anywhere from 2–25 travelers. I've been to two or three of these gatherings and for the most part, have enjoyed them. I've met some people that I have kept in touch with over a long period of time. I've seen listings for people interested in getting together on www.tripadvisor.com, www.craigslist.org, www.fusac.com and www.ricksteves.com.

Use common sense and normal precautions when meeting strangers in Paris.

Many people are interested in taking a cooking class while in Paris. I've never done it, but I have heard positive comments on L'Atelier des Chefs (http://www.atelierdeschefs.com). Be sure to do it in the beginning of the trip so that if you do make friends, you will be able to enjoy each other's company for the duration of your stay.

Another way to meet people is to go where other travelers congregate. For instance, I have always been able to strike up a conversation at Starbucks. Some restaurants like Chartier have communal tables where I have met some interesting people. I have always felt welcome whenever I have attended religious services in Paris.

An American ex-pat, Jim Haynes hosts a dinner at his home for about 50–100 people on Sunday evenings. I attended one night and met quite a few English-speaking guests and made some new friends. Jim is very welcoming and makes guests feel right at home. For details, check his website: www.jim-haynes.com

SIDE TRIPS FROM PARIS

During longer stays in France (more than a week), I like to arrive in Paris and stay for a couple of days. I then embark on a 3–4 day road trip. I usually finish up with a stay in Paris for a few more days. Generally, hotels and B&B's outside of Paris are inexpensive. A resource I use is for places to stay is the *Relais & Châteaux* guide. Website: www.relaischateaux.com. An alternate directory for less expensive but reliable accommodations is *Guides de Charme*. The website is http://www.guidesdecharme. com. I don't normally travel to Paris in the summer, so I have never had trouble finding a place to stay without a reservation, except in Bayeux (near the Normandy invasion beaches).

Here are my favorite side trips from Paris:

- **Loire Valley** – The châteaux here are like something out of a storybook. I took the TGV (high speed train) to Tours, rented a car and spent 2–3 days visiting the fairy-tale castles and sampling the wines. I stayed in châteaux found in the Relais & Châteaux guide. It is easy to enjoy 7 days in the Loire, but a 2 or 3 day trip is doable. My favorite châteaux are Château de Chenonceau, Château de Chambord, Château de Cheverny, Vilandry, and Azey-le-Rideau. A trip to Orléans is worthwhile to examine the history of Joan of Arc. There are no shortages of wineries to visit in the Loire Valley.
- **Normandy** – I drove from Paris to Chartres, Rouen, Mt. Saint-Michel, Dinan, and Honfleur. From there I went to Bayeux from where I visited the Normandy Invasion Beaches and the

American Cemetery. It was a visit that literally changed my life. From there I drove up to Bruges in Belgium for a 2-day stay. I then flew home from Brussels. While in Bayeux, be like the Queen of England or General Eisenhower and stay and dine at the historic Lion d'Or hotel.

- **Champagne Region** – I took a day trip to Reims where I visited the "caves" of all the famous champagne makers like Pommery, Mumm, Piper-Heidseck and Taittinger.

- **Picardy** – This quiet and sleepy region is north of Paris and not widely visited. However, it is beautiful country. I visited Beauvais and the city of Amiens which was frequented by the science-fiction author Jules Verne. The city has an impressive cathedral, larger in size than Notre Dame of Paris. This was a one-night trip and I enjoyed it very much although it was uneventful.

- **Giverney** – The gardens and home of Monet. It can be visited in a day. Get there early before the armada of tour busses arrive. Take the train from Gare Saint-Lazare. It arrives in Vernon in 45 minutes. Then, take the short cab ride or the free bus to Giverney. I describe visiting Giverney as being in a Monet painting as opposed to looking at one. Bring a camera to take photos of the gardens. Photography is not permitted in the house. Closed Mondays and winters. Website: http://giverny.org/gardens

- **The Cathedral at Chartres** – Visit on the way to Normandy or as a day excursion via train. The cathedral is beautiful as well as full of history. Make it a point to take the tour (in English) given by

Malcolm Miller. It can be arranged at the cathedral although he does not give tours in the winter months.

Later in this guide book, I have included further details on how to plan some of these excursions if you wish to undertake them on your own.

OTHER USEFUL INFO

The Métro: When using the Paris métro, you will ask why all other subway systems can't be this good. From any métro station you can get to any other station, rarely with no more than one transfer. When purchasing tickets, buy a "carnet" of 10 at a discounted price of about 11.60 euros. Just say to the clerk at the window, "bonjour, un carnet, s'il vous plâit". The métro closes around 12:30 a.m. during the week and about 1:30 a.m. on weekends. Watch out for pickpockets.

I recall riding the métro for the first time. When I arrived at my destination, the doors did not open up automatically. Luckily, a friendly Parisian showed me that on some métro trains, a latch needs to lifted up on the door in order for it to open.

The Bus: It uses the same tickets as the métro. I especially like the #69 bus which passes through some of the most interesting areas of Paris. Busses use métro tickets to board. Web site for métro and bus: http://www.ratp.fr and here is a link to the route of the #69 bus: http://www.ratp.info/picts/plans/gif/bus_paris/69.gif

The Trains: There are two commuter rail lines in Paris. The métro is like the New York City subway in that it provides transportation within the city. The RER is like the Long Island Railroad and Metro North. It is primarily designed to bring commuters from the suburbs back and forth from Paris. From the train stations or "gares" of the "Grandes Lignes", (the French national train network) high speed TGV and other rail lines to other parts of the country and Europe can be boarded.

Stephen C. Solosky

Sit at the Front of the Boat when Cruising Down Canal St. Martin

When taking a train outside of Paris (other than the RER), tickets must be validated. This is done by stamping it in the yellow machine before boarding. Passengers holding unstamped tickets risk being fined if confronted by an inspector.

The Neighborhoods: I very much like the Latin Quarter/St. Germain des-Prés area along boulevard St. Germain on the left bank. It has a residential, non-touristy ambiance about it. It is very easy to get to the Notre Dame area, Louvre, Orsay and many other attractions from here. The rue de Buci marketplace has good breakfast places, supermarkets, wine shops, etc. Near the Odéon métro station is a Starbucks (yes, Starbucks) where it is easy to run into a lot of Americans to chat with. Generally, I stay away from Champs-Élysées. Some may find it worth a visit, but it is too much like Times Square for me, whereas the Latin Quarter/St. Germain area has more of a "village" feeling.

The Supermarkets: Save money by buying things like bottled water, wine, snacks, and personal items at local supermarkets instead of from your hotel or vendors in tourist areas. Monoprix, Franprix and Carrefour supermarkets are my favorites. Note that supermarkets are usually closed or have limited hours on Sundays.

The Taxis: It is not customary to hail a taxi in Paris. Catch one at a taxi stand or have the hotel or restaurant call one for you. The minimum fare is 6 euros. If a taxi is called from a remote location, the flag is dropped when the taxi is dispatched, not when it picks you up.

The Hotels: Don't assume your hotel has A/C, is non-smoking, has an en suite shower and toilet, has an elevator, or offers internet service. It never hurts to ask questions. Before booking a hotel, inquire if there will be renovations or construction going on inside or outside of the hotel during the time of your planned stay.

The Phones: Get an international phone card before departing for Paris. Better yet, if bringing a laptop computer, download and use Skype to make calls.

The Clocks: In Europe, the 24-hour clock is the convention for indicating the time of day. In North America, this is commonly referred to as "military time". When using a Paris railway timetable for instance, 8:15 means 8:15 a.m. 15:45 converts to 3:45 p.m. and 20:15 indicates a time of 8:15 p.m.

The Airports: The RER is the most reliable method of getting back and forth to the airport. There is nothing more frustrating than getting stuck in a 2-hour traffic jam (believe me, it happens) when your flight leaves in an hour-and-a-half. The moral of the story is to take the RER back to the airport if you absolutely, positively must be on time.

The Strikes: Every now and then, out of the blue, French workers go on strike. I have been in Paris when transport workers were on strike for a day. On another trip, college professors and students demonstrated in the streets. On a third occasion, police needed to disburse a crowd using tear gas. In any case, none of these events were serious enough to significantly disrupt my trip. Job actions and demonstrations are almost always peaceful and they can last for as little as a few hours or they can extend for weeks. However, it would be prudent to keep a safe distance from protests and demonstrations should one be encountered.

The Toilets: In Paris, a restroom is known as a "toilette". It's also called the "W.C." (pronounced "vay-say") as in "water closet". Asking for the bathroom will probably result in nothing but a blank stare. Some public toilettes are co-ed or do not offer the same privacy as might be found in the U.S. Over 400 stand-alone public toilettes (aka sanisettes) can found on the streets if you dare to use one.

Department stores and some métro stations have toilettes. It is customary to tip the attendant who keeps them clean. If using the W.C. in a café or casual restaurant, a security code may be required to enter.

An unsung value of the Museum Pass is that it grants quick, free access to any of 60 or so museums and monuments scattered throughout the city, each one of them with their own clean facilities.

DANGERS AND WARNINGS

Paris is generally a safe city. Take the normal precautions you would take when traveling anywhere else. However, watch out for pickpockets and scam artists. Unfortunately, Paris is full of them. They prey on tourists, particularly the ones who look a bit tired or disoriented, especially as they travel from the airport. I advise keeping valuables in a safe place. Don't trust anyone who wants to give you something for free or tries to put jewelry or clothes on you. Don't be victimized by the scammer who drops change on the bus or asks you to hold something for them. If approached on the street by someone who asks if you speak English, ignore them. A trick I learned from my old days in Brooklyn: keep your wallet in your front pants pocket with a thick rubber band around it. Why? Have you ever tried to pull a wallet out of your pocket with a thick rubber band around it?

Make a color photocopy of your passport and keep it in a safe place. Better yet, scan the copy of the passport and e-mail it to yourself so you can get the copy in an emergency. When I am out for the day in Paris, I leave most of my valuables in the room safe and take only the cash needed for the day, a piece of ID, and a credit card.

Watch your step. A lot of Parisians don't clean up after their dogs.

WHAT TO DO IF YOU LOSE YOUR PASSPORT AND/OR CREDIT CARDS

Although this has never happened to me, I know of people who it has happened to.

As previously mentioned, make copies of your passport and credit cards before departing on your trip. Take these copies along or e-mail them to yourself.

Then, if you lose your credit cards, call the banks immediately and report them as stolen. They will give further instructions for having them replaced. Most major international banks will replace them within 24 hours.

If your passport is lost, report to the U.S. embassy located at the Place de la Concorde, close to the Hôtel de Crillon. The address is 4, avenue Gabriel (Métro: Concorde). The phone number is 01.43.12.22.22. Bring any documents and anyone who can identify you. The website (http://france.usembassy.gov/) also has other resources for things like attorneys, medical service, and emergency numbers.

WHERE TO STAY

As I said, I like staying in the Latin Quarter/Saint Germain des-Près area. The zone near the Louvre near the Tuileries gardens and along rue de Rivoli and rue de Castiglione is fine if you have the money. Regardless of class, almost all Paris hotel rooms are smaller than what is found in the U.S. Not every hotel, even the better ones, have A/C. I avoid large corporate owned hotels.

Paris hotels are government graded as:

- **No stars** – you don't want to stay here.
- **1 Star** – probably no private bath. No A/C. You probably don't want to stay here either.
- **2 Star** – the better ones have private baths and are clean and comfortable. An interior decorator has probably never seen the inside of these hotels. Good ones have hair dryers, elevators, but maybe not A/C. Don't book a 2-star unless it comes recommended to you. 80–125 euros.
- **3 Star** – small, charming hotels. Private bath. 125–200 euros. Usually a safe bet.
- **4 Star** – good hotels. "Business class". 185–275 euros.
- **4 Star luxe and 5 Star** – The Ritz, Meurice, Costes, Lotti, Intercontinental, etc. Some of the best luxury hotels in the world. 275–500 euros.

My picks, listed by star ranking:

Hôtel du College de France – Basic, but a clean, comfortable and quiet 2 star hotel in the Latin Quarter.

I have stayed here before and on my next trip, I am staying here again. Website: http://www.hotel-collegedefrance.com

Hôtel Saint Pierre – In the Latin Quarter. 2-star. A superb location compensates for its lack of charm. I did not stay here personally but I have visited friends at this hotel on two occasions. The hotel is basic, but it is clean, comfortable and quiet. Some rooms have A/C. Website: http://www.saintpierre-hotel.com/uk

Hôtel St. Jacques – A 2-star hotel with a bit of charm located in the Latin Quarter close to the Panthéon. Although it was recently renovated, the rates are still attractive. The movie "Charade" with Cary Grant and Audrey Hepburn was shot here. Website: http://www.hotel-saintjacques.com/en/confort_en.htm

Hôtel de Fleurie – A charming, romantic, and friendly well situated 3-star hotel off boulevard Saint Germain in the St. Germain des-Près area. I like this hotel very much. I have met people who stay here every time they come to Paris. Website: http://www.fleurie-hotel-paris.com

Hôtel Chopin – This is a delightful, old-fashioned and basic 2-star hotel located in a pedestrian arcade at 46, passage Jouffroy in the 9th arrondissement. It is like taking a step back in time. The hotel is located amongst antique shops and quaint boutiques in a lovely part of Paris. Very reasonable rates. Website: http://www.hotelchopin.fr

Hôtel Résidence Foch – Located on a quiet, residential street in the 16th arrondissement away from the center of town, this is the place to stay for those looking for a relaxing sleep. The rooms are small but decorated with sophistication and taste. I have never stayed in a hotel where the personal attention and service has been better. It is a top value for a 3-star hotel. Website: http://www. foch-paris-hotel.com

Hôtel Hospitel Dieu – It is uniquely located on the top floor of a hospital. It is situated in the heart of Paris on the Île de la Cité in the shadow of the Notre-Dame cathedral. Quasimodo's bells will awaken you each morning. It is rated as a 3-star hotel although I thought it was more of a 2-star. The staff is attentive. Since it is in a hospital, all the rooms are smoke free and it is extremely quiet and clean. The price is right, too. Website: http://www.hotel-hospitel. com/ang/accueil.htm

Hôtel Lutetia – A quality 4-star left bank hotel in a top location with views of the Eiffel Tower. It is a good choice for a honeymoon, anniversary, or special occasion. Website: http://www.lutetia-paris.com

Hôtel Mayfair – 4 stars. I have visited friends while they stayed at this hotel. It is in a good location near the Place Vendôme. It is clean, comfortable and it is priced right for a hotel of its class. It is often featured in packages offered by tour companies. It is situated between the Place de la Concorde and the Place Vendôme. Website: http://www. paris-hotel-mayfair.com

Le Grand Intercontinental – A 4-star luxe hotel near the Opéra Garnier. I loved it here when it was .92 euro to the dollar. Join their "club" and get upgraded rooms and use of their "club" floor. Website: www.interconti.com

On a recent trip to Paris, I rented an apartment via the Internet. I don't advise doing this unless you are well-acquainted with Paris. There is no concierge or desk attendant to ask the simplest of questions. If not familiar with the apartment location, you may find yourself in an undesirable locale or in a noisy area. However, when renting an apartment, I advocate renting one that comes with a recommendation from someone who has stayed there.

It is not uncommon for apartments to come without air conditioning or with portable heaters. Elevators might not be found in apartment buildings, particularly older ones. When renting an apartment, you are sending a deposit to someone you almost certainly don't know, so a good amount of trust is involved in the transaction. I sometimes find that apartment owners are willing to negotiate on rental price. For instance, in February (off-season), I bargained a rate 60% off the owner's asking price.

There are other hotels that have come highly recommended to me. I have not stayed in any of these. However, my reliable sources testify that they are charming, clean, comfortable, and a good value.

Here is the list:

Hôtel Sévigné, 2 stars. 2, Rue Mahler, 4th arrondissement. Website: http://www.le-sevigne.com

Hôtel de Nice, 2 stars. 42 bis, rue de Rivoli; 4th arrondissement. Website: www.hoteldenice.com
Hôtel des Grandes Écoles, 75, rue Cardinal Lemoine; the

5th arrondissement. Website: www.hotel-grandes-ecoles.
com

Hôtel Verneuil, 3 stars. 8, rue de Verneuil;
7th arrondissement. Website: www.hotelverneuil.com

Hôtel Muguet, 2 stars. 11, rue Chevert;
7th arrondissement. Website: www.hotelmuguet.com

Hôtel du Champ de Mars, 2 stars. 7, rue du Champ
de Mars; 7th arrondissement. Website: http://www.
hotelduchampdemars.com

Hôtel de Varenne, 3 stars. 44, rue de Bourgogne;
7th arrondissement. Website: www.varenne-hotel-paris.com

New Orient Hôtel, 2 stars. 16, rue de Constantinople;
8th arrondissement. Website: www.hotel-paris-orient.com

Hôtel Langlois, 2 stars. 63, rue Saint-Lazare;
9th arrondissement. Website: www.hotel-langlois.com

Hôtel Windsor Home, 2 stars. 3, rue Vital;
16th arrondissement. Website: www.windsorhomeparis.fr

PARIS WITH CHILDREN

There are some noteworthy options for children in and around Paris. My experience tells me there are a couple of things to keep in mind when traveling with youngsters. First, don't be over-ambitious by doing too much in a day. Second, I found that it is good to negotiate with children in terms of making the trip pleasurable for all parties involved. For instance, strike a deal by saying "Today we will go to the Musée Rodin but tomorrow we will spend the day at Disney".

Stephen C. Solosky

A Visit to Disneyland Paris is Enjoyable for Kids and Adults

Here are my top picks for children's attractions:

Disneyland Resort Paris RER "A"
Disneyland Resorts Paris consists of two parks. Disneyland Park is similar to the Magic Kingdom in Walt Disney World Florida. Walt Disney Studios Park is similar to Walt Disney's Hollywood Studios. Although the French parks are smaller and have a bit less magic than their Florida counterparts, they are enjoyable. Most everything is in English or translated into English. There are some attractions that are not found in the U.S. Most notable is the *CinéMagique* theater show mixing live actors with a synchronized big-screen movie presentation. Be aware that some attractions like Armageddon, may be terrifying to young children. But all in all, a day trip to the park is a good time.

Tickets cost about 60 euros each for adults to enter both parks. Snacks and beverages are not ridiculously expensive nor are they particularly good. The RER A train ride to the park takes about an hour from the center of Paris. Website: http://www.disneylandparis.co.uk

La Cité des Sciences et de l'Industrie
Métro: Porte de la Villette
This is the largest science museum in Europe. It is a worthwhile trip for both children and grown-ups. Many exhibits are interactive. There are exhibits focusing on children from 2–7 years of age as well as those that appeal to all other age groups. I enthusiastically recommend this visit. Website: http://www.cite-sciences.fr/english

Palais de la Découverte

Métro: Champs Elysées-Clemenceau or
Franklin-D.-Roosevelt

This museum centers on six areas: Mathematics,
Astronomy, Geosciences, Physics, Life Sciences, and
Chemistry. It is interesting but not quite as well done
as the Cité des Sciences et de l'Industrie. There are also
fewer explanations in English. However, there is a good
observatory/planetarium. Website: http://www.palais-
decouverte.fr

The Museum of Natural History

Métro: Jussieu or Austerlitz

This museum is located in the beautiful Jardin des Plantes.
It has quite impressive permanent exhibitions on minerals,
paleontology, plants, and evolution. Recent special
presentations have been on whales, the Antarctic, and
North American geology. Website: http://www.mnhn.fr

Bateaux Les Vedettes du Pont-Neuf

Métro: Cité or Pont-Neuf

An hour-long trip up and down the Seine is bound to
entertain anyone. It leaves from the tip of Île de la
Cité directly under the Pont-Neuf. The cost is about
10 euros with a discount coupon obtained at:
http://www.vedettesdupontneuf.com/billet_en.php

TRAVELER'S RESOURCES

- www.tripadvisor.com – the best source anywhere for getting great info on any Paris topic. I cannot emphasize enough how helpful this website is in planning a trip. Of particular value are the message boards where just about any type of Paris travel question can be asked. The user reviews of hotels, attractions, and restaurants are usually unbiased and right on the mark.
- www.ratp.fr – métro and bus maps
- Official Paris tourist website: http://en.parisinfo. com.
- My website, www.travelingprofessor.com.
- The *New York Times* keeps an archive of its excellent travel articles including neighborhood descriptions, restaurant, and hotel reviews. Registration may be required, but it's free. Website: www.nytimes.com.
- A handy guide for choosing a restaurant is *Eating and Drinking in Paris* by Andy Herbach and Michael Dillon. The menu translator provides invaluable help for navigating through a French menu.

CDG (CHARLES DEGAULLE) AIRPORT – THE INS AND OUTS

The airport is drab, not well laid-out, and the food services are less than average. It is consistently cited as one of the worst airports in Europe.

Most overseas flights arrive at Terminal 2. Others go to Terminal 1.

Upon arrival to CDG, I have never had my belongings checked by customs, but it is always necessary to go through passport control. It takes about 20 minutes after disembarking the plane to get through passport control. Another 15–30 minutes or so is needed to retrieve checked bags.

Here are the transportation options to/from the airport:

Taxi

At the airport, get a taxi at one of the taxi stands. Don't be afraid to ask other travelers if they would like to share a taxi into town. Fares can range from 38 euros (no traffic at all) to 75 euros or more if you are waiting in a lot of traffic. During heavy traffic, it might take 2 hours to get to/from CDG and the meter is running the entire time. There is an additional charge of a euro per bag for two or more bags. A taxi is a good option if you have a few pieces of heavy luggage. Only take a taxi from a taxi stand that is clearly marked as such.

By the way, I frequently have been in taxis that had the smell of tobacco smoke.

Bus

There are two bus options:

Roissybus (http://www.ratp.info/informer/anglais/
aeroport_roissybus.php):

Travels between CDG and Paris Opéra Garnier (rue
Scribe and rue Auber). It takes 45–60 minutes. It runs
every 15 minutes between 6 a.m. – 7 p.m. and every
20 minutes between 7 p.m. – 11 p.m. Cost: 8.90 euros.
Then, take a taxi/métro/bus from Opéra Garnier to
your final destination.

Air France Bus (http://transfer.airport-paris.com/air-
france-coach-service.htm):

There are 2 routes to/from CDG:

**Route #2: CDG->Porte Maillot->Arc de
Triomphe.** Cost: 13 euros 1 way, 20 euros return
(R/T).

Route #4: CDG->Gare de Lyon->Montparnasse.
Cost: 14 euros 1 way, 22 euros return (R/T).

There are signs in the airport designating Air France
Bus pick up points. They are located close to gates
B1 and C2. Pay the driver in euros upon boarding the
bus. Travelers with heavy luggage, disabled persons, or
families with small children in tow may find this option
to be uncomfortable.

Private Shuttle

There are a variety of private shuttle operators at CDG.
They usually use chauffeur–driven vans or min-vans that

will take you directly to your hotel, sometimes with stops in-between. The cost for a single person is usually about 30 euros with further discounts depending upon the number of people in your party. It is important to make reservations with a shuttle service prior to departing on your trip. Make certain to have a firm agreement on the price before contracting with a private shuttle company. Shuttles are good options for people with heavy luggage and/or limited mobility.

RER Train

This is probably the cheapest, fastest, and most reliable choice. The trains run about every 15 minutes from 5 a.m. until about midnight. It is 8.40 euros (5.80 for children 4–10). The express trip is about 22 to 30 minutes, depending upon your destination.

Route: CDG Terminal 2->CDG Terminal 1-> Gare du Nord-> Châtelet-Les Halles->St-Michel-Notre Dame->Luxembourg->Port Royal->Denfert-Rochereau

Upon arriving at CDG, take the 10 minute walk down to the direction of the "gare" (train station). There is a shuttle bus but it isn't worth waiting for and dragging your luggage on and off. Go downstairs and look for a ticket office with a line of other travelers waiting. You will see other people purchasing tickets at the ticket kiosk, but unless your credit card has a computer chip in it (American credit cards don't have these), you cannot buy a ticket at the kiosk. Purchase a one-way or return RER ticket to Paris. The ticket is valid for a ride to the RER terminal in Paris and a métro ride (if necessary) to your destination. Hold onto the ticket, it may be needed to exit the station.

The upside of taking the RER is that it is cheap, reliable, and quick way to get into the city. The downside is that there is some walking and escalators/stairs involved. For those with heavy luggage, it may not be a good choice. Sometimes on the RER, beggars and buskers can be encountered.

Departing for the U.S. involves checking bags and going through security. The whole process takes about 40 minutes or less. I get to the airport about 2 hours before departure.

Several years ago, the ATM's in the airport never worked or were constantly out of money. That problem seems to have been corrected. ATM's in the city work fine. Make sure there is money in your checking account in order to use a bank card. Bring a back-up card in case of emergency.

JET LAG

Considering:

- Most flights from the U.S. to Paris are overnight flights.
- For a good portion of the year, there is at least a 6 hour time difference between the U.S. and Paris. For instance, if it is 8 a.m. in Paris, it is 2 a.m. in New York.
- Today's air travel environment is exhausting, stressful, and uncomfortable.

This all adds up to a serious case of jet lag for some travelers.

I have an acquaintance who is an international flight attendant, and this is her advice to assuage jet lag:

- Sleep in your own comfortable bed as late as possible until it is time to leave for the airport.
- Take a nap of about an hour or two on the plane.
- Have no more than 1 or 2 alcoholic beverages during the flight.
- Drink plenty of water on the flight.
- Upon arriving in Paris, grab something to eat, go to the hotel and try to nap again for a couple of hours.
- Upon awakening, get right on Paris time. For instance, if you normally eat dinner at 7 p.m. at home, eat dinner at 7 p.m. in Paris. If you regularly retire at 11 p.m. at home, go to bed at 11 p.m. in Paris.

DAILY TRAVEL ITINERARIES

Most people plan to visit sites in Paris according to proximity to each other. For instance, they will visit the Latin Quarter on one day and perhaps Montmartre another. However, a thematic touring plan can be very interesting and quite fun.

Here are my favorite daily itineraries:

Itinerary #1: Your First Day in Paris
Here is an itinerary to get started on the right foot when visiting Paris for the first time. It helps familiarize you with the city and gets you to see some great sites right away.

You will:

- Use the métro.
- Get a general idea of the layout of the city.
- Visit Notre Dame Cathedral.
- Walk along the Seine to the Tuileries Garden past the Louvre.
- View the Eiffel Tower and the Musée d'Orsay.
- Cross the Seine and walk through St. Germain des-Prés and the Latin Quarter.
- Have your first Paris café experience.

Most international flights land in the morning at CDG airport. Try to take care of some business at the terminal. Withdraw some euros from the ATM if possible. Pick up a Museum Pass at the orange "Touriste Information" booth at the airport.

Upon touching down in Paris, you may or may not have jet lag. In any case, adrenaline will sustain the excitement of your first day. Get over to the hotel, check in and drop your luggage. Take a nap if possible. You'll have at least half a day to get a general familiarization of the layout and transportation system of Paris.

The best place to start your excursion is right smack in the middle of Paris in front of the Notre Dame Cathedral. It is truly the center of France as indicated by the brass "Paris Point Zero" marker, the point from which all distances in France are measured.

To get to Notre Dame, get on the métro (see the section on "Transportation") and head towards the Cité métro station. As you climb out of the underground, you will be a bit disoriented. However, some short steps one way or another you will recognize the towers of Notre Dame.

Walk in the direction of the towers to the plaza in front of the Cathedral. It is known as the "Parvis". When standing on the Parvis facing away from the cathedral, notice that you are on an island. On the left across the river is the left bank where the Latin Quarter is. On the other side is the right bank, of course.

Take a visit inside the cathedral. There is no admission charge. When leaving, walk away from Notre Dame and cross the first bridge on the left, Petit Pont. You are now on the left bank. Walk along the Seine. Notice the "bouqinistes" selling their ancient books and magazines from their metal stands. It's a great photo op. Walk down past the Pont Saint-Michel along the Seine. The next bridge is Pont-Neuf. Crossing over it, there is a spectacular view of the Eiffel Tower. By the way, at this point you can walk down the stairs to the point of Île de la Cité and take one of the Bateaux Vedettes du Pont-Neuf which is a boat ride that provides a lovely tour up and down the Seine. I suggest it to give your legs a rest and relax and enjoy the cruise.

Otherwise, continue walking until you arrive on the right bank. Make a left and continue walking down the Seine. The massive Musée de Louvre greets you on the right. Keep walking past the Pont des Arts, Pont du Carrousel, and Pont Royal. On the right will be the Tuileries Gardens.

Cross the Seine again at the next footbridge. Again, get a spectacular look at the Eiffel Tower. After crossing the Seine make a left. Pass the Musée d'Orsay and walk back towards Notre Dame.

When you get back to Petit Pont, carefully cross the street and look for the Café Petit Pont. It's the perfect spot for a café au lait and a divine view of Notre Dame.

Itinerary #2: Offbeat Paris
Paris has glamorous attractions like the Eiffel Tower, Louvre, and the Cathedral of Notre Dame. However, after you've seen all the touristy stuff, it's time to do something out of the ordinary. Take a look at this plan of attack for a truly unusual experience.

Start the day at the Sewers of Paris (les Égouts de Paris) located in the shadow of the Eiffel Tower. It's an hour-long sub-surface walking tour of a small part of the

1,300 miles that make up the Paris underground sewer system. Don't worry about this tour being a stinker, it is quite entertaining. It is one tour that, literally, can be enjoyed rain or shine. When the weather is wet, the sewers flow like rapids. When it's hot and sunny, it's cool and breezy deep inside. Métro: Alma-Marceau. Museum Pass: Yes
Website: http://www.parismuseumpass.com/en/musees_infos_pratiques.php?musee_id=23

Next, get on the métro at Invalides for a 30–40 minute ride to the outside environs of Paris for a date with history at the Basilique Saint-Denis. It is situated on the burial place of virtually all of the kings and queens of France since Clovis in 511. During the French revolution, many of the buried bodies were unceremoniously dug up and placed in a mass grave on the site, but the monuments still remain. In any case, it is the final resting place of monarchs such as Marie Antoinette and Louis XVI. Don't miss the mummified remains of the dauphin (prince) who would have been Louis XVII. If you like the macabre, this is the place to be. Get the audio guide – it will greatly enhance the visit. Métro: Basilique de Saint-Denis. Museum Pass: Yes
Website: http://saint-denis.monuments-nationaux.fr/en/?fl_r=11

The next stop on this "I See Dead People" tour is the famous Père Lachaise cemetery located at the métro station of the same name. It is the final vacation spot of luminaries such as Jim Morrison, Max Ernst, Edith Piaf, and many more. Be sure to visit the cemetery's website or get hold of a map in order to plan the visit. The best place to buy the map is at the cemetery entrance nearest the métro station. The grounds are widespread and the hilly paths are winding and made up

of cobblestones. No admission fee is required. Website: http://
www.pere-lachaise.com

Next, a visit to the Catacombs, located near the
Denfert-Rochereau métro station is as off-beat as
can be. When the cemeteries of central Paris became
overcrowded and unsanitary in the 1700's, they carted off
the remains of over six million skeletons and placed them
in this underground ossuary. Bring a flashlight and watch
your head. They will check to make sure you didn't take
along any "souvenirs" upon exiting the Catacombs. There
is an admission charge of about 7 euros not covered by the
Museum Pass. Website: http://www.catacombes-de-paris.fr/
english.htm

If it is a Sunday night, check out the legendary Jim
Haynes dinner at his private residence. It's within walking
distance of the Catacombs or take the métro to the
Alesia station. Usually he gets an eclectic bunch of 75–100
people to show up. Half of them are French but the other
half are travelers just like you. To get an invite, check out
his website, http://www.jim-haynes.com

Itinerary #3: Whirlwind Paris in a Day or Two
What if you only have a day or two to visit Paris? What
should you see? Where should you go?

Here is my itinerary for a quick visit to see the highlights
of Paris:

Cathedral of Notre Dame/Île Saint-Louis
Métro: Cité
Over 10 million people visit the Cathedral of Notre Dame
every year, so why shouldn't you? Admission is free to the
cathedral itself. If there is a line to get inside, it usually

moves quickly. However, there is usually a long and slow queue to climb the towers. Opt to skip that part if time is short. A visit to the cathedral on Île de la Cité is the perfect place to get your bearings and visit the center of Paris. Behind the cathedral is the Pont Saint-Louis leading to the charming Île Saint Louis.

Museé de Louvre
Métro: Louvre
Don't leave Paris without a smile from Mona. However, strategize a visit to the Louvre carefully. It is the largest museum in the world and it is easy wander aimlessly unless you have a plan for your visit. The Louvre is open every day but Tuesday. It is open late on Wednesday and Fridays. Prioritize what you wish to see. Most visitors look for these masterpieces: Mona Lisa, Venus de Milo, Nike (Winged Victory of Samothrace), the Coronation of Napoleon (painting) and the Greek & Etruscan sculptures. There is an excellent website to help plan thematic tours of the Louvre with specific directions: http://www.louvre.fr/llv/activite/liste_parcours.jsp?bmLocale=en

Champs-Élysées and Arc de Triomphe
Métro: Charles de Gaulle – Étoile
If time permits, walk through the Tuileries Gardens to the Concorde Métro station. Otherwise hop on board the métro directly to the Franklin Delano Roosevelt station and walk the Champs-Élysées to the Arc de Triomphe. Take the underground tunnels to get to the Arc de Triomphe itself. Climb to the top and get a panoramic view of Paris.

Seine Cruise
After dinner, take a cruise on the Bateaux Vedettes du Pont-Neuf. It departs from the tip of Île de la Cité at Pont-Neuf. You'll see why they call Paris the "City of Light".

Another option is to cruise on the Bateaux Mouches from the Pont de l'Alma, across from the Eiffel Tower.

Café Petit Pont

For a nightcap, take an outdoor table at the Café Petit Pont for a million euro view while listening to some light music or jazz, all for the price of a glass of wine.

Stephen C. Solosky

Place du Tertre is in the Heart of Montmartre

If You Have a 2nd Day:

Montmartre/Basilique du Sacré-Cœur/Place de Tertre

Métro: Abbesses

This tour gives a taste of Paris just as you think it would be. Métro it to the Abbesses station and walk to the base of the hill of the basilica. Take the funicular to the top and get a fantastic view of the city. Around the corner is

Montmartre's Place du Tertre. It is a square full of cafés and portrait artists. To many people, this is the heart of Paris.

Rodin Museum/Napoleon's Tomb
Métro: Varenne or Invalides
These two sites are conveniently close. Long known for its sculpture garden, the Rodin Museum also houses other fine works of art. Practically across the street is the domed Napoleon's Tomb. For World War II buffs, the adjacent Musée de l'Armée is not to be missed.

Marais
Métro: St-Paul
A métro ride to the St-Paul station on métro line #1 drops you off in the colorful Marais section of Paris. Take away a falafel at L'As du Fallafel on rue des Rosiers and walk to the Picasso museum. After that, visit Victor Hugo's home at Place des Vosges. Drop in on the art galleries surrounding the square.

And, if time permits:

Musée d'Orsay: located on the left bank of the Seine between Île de la Cité and Place de Concorde. It is open late on Thursdays.

L'Orangerie: home of Monet's Water Lilies is located in the Tuileries adjacent to the Place de Concorde. It is an easy walk from the Musée d'Orsay.

Itinerary #4: Fashion Tour of Paris
Sometimes I think the city of Paris is a fashion show unto itself. It seems that Parisians have been born with a sense of style and panache. For instance, observe how the

French women wear scarves. Notice how the children are neatly attired. French men can dress casually and still seem to have that sophisticated sense of style.

Here is my itinerary for fashion lovers:

Avenue Montaigne
With shops and boutiques paying rents approaching $55,000 per square meter, this is one of the wealthiest (and fashionable) streets in the world. Start at the location of the Franklin D. Roosevelt metró station and spend your way down the "Miracle Half-Mile" down towards the Alma-Marceau métro station. On the way, notice the legendary names of fashion on the shops of Bulgari, Dior, Chanel, Valentino, Ferragamo, Celine, Nina Ricci and more. There are clothes, handbags, accessories, and shoes that would make Carrie Bradshaw blush. Speaking of Carrie Bradshaw, stop at the Hôtel Plaza Athénée, site of the last episode of "Sex and the City" and have a (pricey) Cosmopolitan with lunch.

Galleries Lafayette Department Store
Metro: Chaussée d'Antin – La Fayette
This famous *grands magasin* (department store) is located at 40, boulevard Haussmann. Each week they feature a 30-minute fashion show on Friday at 3 p.m. There is commentary in English. Reservations are a must and should be done early. They can be obtained by e-mail at welcome@galerieslafayette.com.

Afterwards, do a runway walk over to Le Printemps, just down the block at 64, boulevard Haussmann. Web sites: http://www2.galerieslafayette.com/international/goFolder.do?f=home_en&lang=en and http://departmentstoreparis.printemps.com.

Les Arts Décoratifs

Métro: Palais Royal – Musée du Louvre

This is the museum of French lifestyle, located in a wing
of the Louvre. Two of the collections housed here
are of special attention to those interested in fashion.
The decorative arts collection is dedicated to the
understanding of the evolution of human taste, style and
crafts. The fashion and textile museum presents temporary
exhibits concerned with the history of garments. A famous
designer is often asked to participate in the design of these
exhibitions. Website: http://www.lesartsdecoratifs.fr

Musée Galliera

Metro: Iléna

This museum was seen in the film, "The Devil Wears
Prada". It is the fashion museum of Paris. All of its
exhibits are temporary. Sometimes a top name in fashion
is featured. At other times there might be an exhibit on
a fashion era, or perhaps a certain fashion theme will be
promoted. The museum is open every day but Monday
and whenever there is a scheduled exhibit. Therefore, it
is important to check the website before going: http://
en.parisinfo.com/museum-monuments/294/musee-galliera-
musee-de-la-mode-de-la-ville-de-paris

Check this website for a comprehensive listing of the top
Paris fashion sites:
http://www.stargonaut.com/fashion.html

Itinerary #5: Science & Technology

Paris' achievements and exhibitions in science, technology,
and engineering have long been overshadowed by its other
charms. However, at one time, Paris was the center of the
industrial and scientific universe. The exhibits in science,

technology, and engineering are amongst the best in the world.

La Cité des Sciences et de l'Industrie
Métro: Porte de la Villette
This is one of the largest and most impressive science and industry museums in the world. It is modern, entertaining, informative, and interactive. Children and adults alike will be astounded. I highly recommend a visit to this museum. Closed Monday. Website: http://www.cite-sciences.fr/english

One could spend at least a day at this museum and the surrounding park. But a great idea is to take a relaxing mid-day cruise down Napoleon's Canal St. Martin to Place Bastille. Website: http://www.canauxrama.com/e_index.html

Musée des Arts et Métiers
Métro: Arts et Métiers or Réaumur-Sébastopol
Not as entertaining as la Cité des Sciences et de l'Industrie. However, it is filled with fascinating historical artifacts of science, technology, architecture, and science. This is truly a hidden gem of Paris and to those who have any interest at all in technology, engineering, and science. Closed Monday. Website: http://www.arts-et-metiers.net

Palais de la Découverte
Métro: Champs Elysées-Clemenceau or Franklin-D.-Roosevelt
Geared more towards students, it is located right off the Champs-Élysées, this. There are exhibits on Astronomy, Physics, Mathematics, Chemistry, Geosciences, Life Sciences, and Astrophysics.

Musée de l'Informatique
Métro: La Défense
In short, it is an exhibit on the history of computing. There are displays of old computing devices and an exhibit on the history of the Internet and the World Wide Web. There are also stunning views of Paris from the top of the Grande Arche. Website: http://www.museeinformatique.fr

Other sites of interest:

Museé de Radio de France (French Radio Museum): http://www.paris.org/Musees/Radio.France
Le Observatoire de Paris: http://www.obspm.fr/presentation.en.shtml
Musée de l'Air et de l'Espace (Air and Space Museum): http://www.mae.org
Institut Henri Poincare: http://www.ihp.jussieu.fr

TRIPS OUTSIDE OF PARIS

Transportation systems and highways in France (and throughout Europe, for the most part) are excellent. A trip of a day or two outside Paris is relatively easy to arrange. Lodging outside of major cities is also generally inexpensive, except during special events or holiday periods.

When driving in Europe, check with your auto insurance company regarding coverage.

Here are my favorite short trips outside of Paris:

Château de Versailles
Versailles is the most opulent of all French châteaux. It is closed on Mondays. Avoid visiting on weekends and on Tuesdays – it can get overly crowded.

Getting to the home of Marie Antoinette is a piece of cake. Start by boarding the "RER-C Rive Gauche" (be careful not to take the "RER-C Saint Quentin") train. This requires a separate RER ticket purchase at about 3 euros each way. Remember to hold onto your ticket for the entire trip, as it is needed to exit the train station. Buy tickets from a clerk at the RER station when you plan to travel. No reservations are necessary.

Trains to Versailles leave about every 20 minutes and take about half an hour to get there.

Upon arriving at the Versailles train station, just follow the crowds to the château. It is about a 15 minute walk from the train station. I suggest a visit the château be followed by taking the mini-bus over to the Trianon Palaces. Sometimes there are special tours of the private apartments for a separate admission. It will be posted if they are available.

The RER train ticket is flexible in that it is not necessary to take a particular train at a particular time.

Giverney (Home of Monet)

This is a trip not to be missed by those who love Impressionist painting. It involves taking a 45-minute train ride from Gare Saint-Lazare to Vernon. A bus then picks you up at the train station to Giverney, the site of Monet's home. Monet's home at Giverney is open from April through October. It is closed on Mondays.

I strongly suggest taking the early train from Paris (leaves about 8:20 and arrives in Vernon at 9:06). Opt to purchase tickets at Gare Saint-Lazare the day before since my experience has shown me that sometimes there is an hour or more wait at the ticket desk. The automated kiosks don't accept non-European credit cards.

Before boarding the train, validate the train ticket by having it stamped by one of the yellow machines.

Upon arriving in Vernon, look for the (free) bus right outside the train station to the 10-minute journey to Giverney. Taxis are readily available too.

You probably want the 12:53 or 2:53 (14:53) back to Paris from Vernon. Your train ticket will most likely be a "flexible" ticket that allows travel on either train. Tickets are about 40 euros R/T.

The City of Champagne: Reims

Reims is the Champagne city of France. It is the home of some of the most celebrated Champagne makers in the world – Taittinger, Mumm, Pommery, Piper-Hiedsick, and more. There is also the impressive Cathedral of Notre Dame, Reims – the coronation site of most of the kings and queens of France. Also of interest is the Musée de la Reddition (The Surrender Museum), the site of the surrender of the Third Reich to the Allies at the end of WWII. The museum is closed Tuesdays.

Most people choose to board the 8:57 or 11:27 TGV train to Reims from Gare d'Lest. Buy a ticket at the SNCF or "Grandes Lignes" desk at the station. Ask about a "flexible" return ticket if unsure of your return time. That way, a 10 euro service fee to change the ticket is avoided. There is usually not a big crowd at Gare d'lEst, so you can probably buy your ticket on the date of your travel.

The comfortable TGV takes 45 minutes to get to Reims. Before boarding, place the ticket in the yellow machine to validate it. Seats on the TGV are assigned. There is no open seating. Conductors standing outside of the train before it departs are friendly and helpful. They will be happy to answer any questions.

Depending on the day, there are different schedules for return trains. But there is usually a direct train at 4:15 (16:15) and 8:15 (20:15). Connecting trains run more frequently.

Reims is a lovely little city with plenty of restaurants and cafés. The cathedral is within walking distance. To the left side and adjacent to the cathedral is the tourist office. Reservations are mandatory at most champagne houses. The tourist office staff will be glad to assist with reservations and call a taxi for you to get there. You may want to reserve tours online a couple of days beforehand if you are going on a weekend, holiday, or peak tourist time.

I like the Pommery and Taittinger Champagne houses. They each charge a fee of 12–18 euros. Don't hesitate to visit the others.

The well done Reims tourist guide (with a list of Champagne houses, a map, and other activities) can be downloaded here: http://www.reims-tourism.com

Normandy Invasion Beaches

Actually, to do justice to a visit to the Normandy invasion beaches, I advise making this an overnight trip (2 nights for WWII buffs) in the town of Bayeux, about 165 miles from Paris. It is the best location as a command center to tour the Normandy beaches. Because I value my life, I would not drive from inside the city of Paris, but I would take the 2 hour train from Gare Saint-Lazare in Paris to Caen at about $48 each way. One word of warning: during certain times of the year, particularly in early June, it is nearly impossible to get a hotel reservation. At other times, hotels and B&B's go begging for visitors.

I also suggest that you read a book or pick up some literature on the events surrounding June 6, 1944. I advise reading Stephen Ambrose's "D Day: June 6, 1944: The Climactic Battle of World War II" for an in-depth understanding of the invasion and the areas around the invasion beaches. I also advise viewing the DVD's "The Longest Day" and "Saving Private Ryan" in preparation for the trip.

Le Mémorial at Caen is an excellent museum. There are virtually no relics (equipment, debris, etc.) left at the invasion beaches, but many of them are on display here. The website is: http://www.memorial-caen.fr/fr/circuit_tour/index.php?lang=EN

I then recommend renting a car for the 30-minute drive to Bayeux. Check in at the Hôtel Lion d'Or. It is a relatively inexpensive hotel that is rich in charm and history. Its website is http://www.liondor-bayeux.fr. There are many other hotels and B&B's in the area that are affordable and welcoming. Most people speak English in Normandy since it is so close to Britain and because of the large number of English-speaking visitors.

To start the tour of the invasion beaches, I recommend the 40 minute drive from Bayeux to Sainte-Mère-Église, the town depicted in the movie "The Longest Day" where a paratrooper's parachute was caught on the spire of the church. The soldier feigned death until the town was liberated the next day. Others like to start at the closer, bomb-cratered, Pointe du Hoc. This is the place where the 2nd Ranger Battalion scaled the cliffs and overtook a German bunker placement. I was stunned when I saw what these brave men had to overcome to be successful at their task. The brutal opening scenes of "Saving Private Ryan" are based upon the battle at Pointe du Hoc. On the 40th anniversary of the invasion, President Ronald Regan dedicated a memorial there.

Further north, are the Omaha and Gold beaches. There are memorials and remembrances along the way. I can recall encountering some surviving veterans, recognizable by their VFW caps, who were revisiting the beaches. If you wish to speak with them, approach them with care and dignity. It is surely an emotional moment for them. There is no movie, book, or tour guide that can substitute for the stories that these men can tell.

Take your time while driving further along the beaches. If visiting in or about June, take your shoes off and walk into the shallow surf. It will be cold. Imagine how those brave men waded through these then blood-red waters in 1944, with bullets flying from the cliffs and explosions all around them.

The American Cemetery in Colleville-sur-Mer overlooks the cliffs of Omaha Beach. Everyone reacts differently to their visit to this cemetery. However, I can say that I personally do not have the capability to describe my emotions upon seeing the thousands of crosses and Stars of David on that field. It was indeed a day that changed my personal outlook on life forever.

On the 65th anniversary of the invasion, the American Cemetery was the site where President Barack Obama and the leaders of Canada, France, and Great Britain honored those who fought and died in the invasion and liberation of Europe.

It is important to remember that it was not just the Americans who participated in the invasion. There are memorials in honor of all of the forces who were involved in that fateful day.

There is a good museum at Arromanches, the Musée du Débarquement which has some interesting relics, exhibits and multimedia presentations. Website: http://www.musee-arromanches.fr/accueil/index.php?lang=uk

At day's end, Bayeux is the perfect place to chill out, drink some calvados, and enjoy a fine meal.

Another attraction in Bayeaux worthwhile seeing is the famous tapestry depicting the 1066 Normandy invasion of England. Don't pass it up.

All in all, a visit to the Normandy invasion beaches is very worthwhile. But please, don't take a "packaged" tour. It is a place that deserves to be taken at its own pace.

Brussels Day Trip

One my favorite day trips is to take the easy 1 ½ hour train ride up to Brussels (known as *Bruxelles* in French). Trains run frequently from Gare du Nord into Brussels Midi station. The round trip fare is less than $100 if you book in advance.

Brussels is a terrific walking city. It's funky, it's gothic, and the mussels and beer just cannot be beat. Have a Belgian waffle and bring some chocolate home with you. In many ways it is much different than Paris. English is widely spoken. For Brussels tourist info, including a map, try this link: http://www.visitbelgium.com

Here are my recommendations for things to see and do in Brussels:

Grand Place (aka Grote Markt): I love to promenade around the grandest of all squares in Europe. It is surrounded by guild houses, the Hôtel de Ville, and the Musée de la Ville. Each time I visit I discover something new.

Mannekin Pis: This is an irreverent statue of a young boy doing his business. It is certainly not in the class of the Eiffel Tower, but it might be Brussels most famous landmark. Have a chuckle, take a snapshot, and move on.

Musées Royaux des Beaux-Arts (Royal Museums of Fine Arts): This is a fine collection of mostly Belgian art, both historical and contemporary. There are works by such well-known artists as Rubens, Van Dyck, and Rembrandt. Website: http://www.fine-arts-museum.be/site/EN

Chocolate: While strolling the streets off the Grand Place notice the chocolate boutiques sprinkled about. Don't hesitate to sample the goods but don't overdo it, save some room for a Belgian waffle and mussels and beer later. You can always bring some chocolate back to Paris.

Mussels and Beer: Beer is a high art form in Belgium. It is only enhanced when it is paired with mussels (moules) and twice-fried fries (frites). My little slice of heaven for this delight is La Villette. Website: http://www.la-villette.be

TRAVELINGPROFESSOR.COM

The TravelingProfessor.Com website is dedicated to those who love to travel to Paris. It is the companion website to this guide book. The URL is: http://www.travelingprofessor.com. In the public areas of the website travelers will find:

- The Traveling Professor's Paris blog.
- Videos of Paris places of interest.
- A Paris Forum. It's a place to ask questions and get answers on traveling to Paris.
- Classfied Ads. Buy, sell, or trade everything pertaining to Paris.
- Photos albums of trips to Paris and Europe.
- Links to lodging, deals and discounts, articles, reviews, language tutorials, drinking and dining, travel related print articles, and more.
- A free subscription to my monthly Paris newsletter.

Owners of The Traveling Professor's Guide to Paris have VIP access to certain areas of the site:

- Each and every link from this guidebook is listed. Just point and click to get more information. No need to type in the links listed in this guide book.
- Updates to the guide.
- Late-breaking news on special events and happenings in Paris.
- Special deals and discounts available only to those who own "The Traveling Professor's Guide to Paris".

SPECIAL FEATURES

I have taken the entries in this guide and listed them by category. Hopefully, this will give some good ideas for planning your trip.

Most Popular
- Cathédrale de Notre Dame de Paris (Notre Dame Cathedral)
- Eiffel Tower (Tour Eiffel)
- Musée du Louvre
- Sácre-Cœur
- Princess Diana (Unofficial) Memorial
- Centre Pompidou – Musée National d'Art Moderne
- Musée Picasso
- Musée Rodin
- Musée d'Orsay
- Musée de l'Orangerie
- Panthéon
- Arc de Triomphe

Free-No Admission Charge
- American Cathedral in Paris
- Place de la Bastille
- Musée Carnavalet
- Luxembourg Gardens
- Cathédrale de Notre Dame de Paris (Notre Dame Cathedral)
- Pont-Neuf
- Princess Diana (Unofficial) Memorial
- Sácre-Cœur
- Église Saint-Etienne-du-Mont
- Église Saint-Sulpice
- Shakespeare & Company

Tuileries Gardens
Place du Vert Galant
Place des Vosges

Art Exhibits
Musée Carnavalet
National Museum of Asian Art Guimet
Musée du Louvre
Musée Marmottan
Musée de l'Orangerie
Musée d'Orsay
Musée Picasso
Centre Pompidou – Musée National d'Art Moderne
Musée Rodin
Château de Versailles
Place des Vosges
Musée National du Moyen Age – Thermes et Hôtel de
  Cluny (Cluny Museum)
Conciergerie
Panthéon
Sainte-Chapelle
Église Saint-Etienne-du-Mont
Église Saint-Sulpice

Military Exhibits
Arc de Triomphe
Musée de l'Armée (Army Museum)
Musée Carnavalet
Conciergerie
Napoleon's Tomb
Panthéon

Science and Technology
Musée des Arts et Metiers
La Cité des Sciences et de l'Industrie

Musée des Égouts de Paris (Sewers of Paris)
Eiffel Tower (Tour Eiffel)
Palais de la Découverte
Museum of Natural History

Cathedrals, Religious Monuments, Cemeteries, and Memorials

American Cathedral in Paris
Basilique de Saint-Denis (Cathedral Basilica of Saint-Denis)
Cathédrale de Notre Dame de Paris (Notre Dame Cathedral)
Sácre-Cœur
Sainte-Chapelle
Église Saint-Etienne-du-Mont
Église Saint-Sulpice
Pére Lachaise Cemetery
Princess Diana (Unofficial) Memorial
Arc de Triomphe
Panthéon

Music and Performance Art

American Cathedral in Paris
Cathédrale de Notre Dame de Paris (Notre Dame Cathedral)
Opéra Garnier (Palais Garnier)
Sainte-Chapelle
Église Saint-Sulpice

Impressionist Art

Musée Marmottan
Musée d'Orsay
Musée Picasso
Musée Rodin
Musée de l'Orangerie

Place des Vosges
Giverney

A Bit Out of the Way, But Worth It
Musée Marmottan
Père Lachaise Cemetery (Cimetière du Père-Lachaise)
La Cité des Sciences et de l'Industrie
Château de Versailles
Disneyland Resort Paris
Basilique de Saint-Denis (Cathedral Basilica of
    Saint-Denis)
Canal Saint Martin-Canauxrama
Bercy Neighborhood

Restaurants: Chez Michel, Le Buerre Noisette

Near Champs-Élysées Area
American Cathedral in Paris
Eiffel Tower (Tour Eiffel)
Princess Diana (Unofficial) Memorial
Arc de Triomphe
National Museum of Asian Art Guimet
La Defense

Hotel: Hôtel Residence Foch
Shopping: Avenue Montaigne

Near Place de la Concorde
Musée du Louvre
Musée de l'Orangerie
Musée d'Orsay
Tuileries Gardens

Restaurants: L'Ardoise, Angelina
Hotels: Hôtel Mayfair
Shopping: Rue Saint-Honoré

Near Île de la Cité
Cathédrale de Notre Dame de Paris (Notre Dame
    Cathedral)
Bateaux Les Vedettes du Pont-Neuf
Berthillon
Conciergerie
Musée du Louvre
Pont-Neuf
Sainte-Chapelle
Shakespeare & Company
Place du Vert Galant
Île Saint-Louis

Restaurants: Brasserie du Louvre, Les Bouquinistes,
Café Le Petit Pont, Berthillon, Taverne Henri IV Wine
Bar, L'Ecluse Wine Bar
Hotel: Hôtel Hospitel Dieu

Near Latin Quarter/Saint Germain des-Prés
Bateaux les Vedettes du Pont-Neuf
Luxembourg Gardens
Musée d'Orsay
Pont-Neuf
Église Saint-Etienne-du-Mont
Shakespeare & Company
Église Saint-Sulpice
Panthéon
Musée National du Moyen Age – Thermes et Hôtel de
    Cluny (Cluny Museum)

Street Markets: Marché Raspail, Mouffetard, Buci Market
Shopping: Le Bon Marché Department Store
Restaurants: Brasserie Lipp, Le Pré Verre, Le Coupe Chou, A La Petite Chaise, Les Bouquinistes, Les Éditeurs, Café Le Petit Pont, Pâtisserie Viennoise, Bistrot d'Henri, Au Beaujolais, L'Ecluse Wine Bar
Hotels: Hôtel de Fleurie, Hôtel Lutetia, Hôtel St. Jacques, Hôtel St. Pierre, Hôtel du College de France, Hôtel des Grandes Écoles

Near Opéra Area
Opéra Garnier (Palais Garnier)

Restaurants: Chartier, Aux Lyonnais, Racines Wine Bar
Hotels: Hôtel Chopin, Le Grande Intercontinental
Shopping: Galleries Lafayette, Au Printemps

Stephen C. Solosky

Rue Cler is a Favorite Spot for Travelers

Near Eiffel Tower

Bateaux Mouches
Eiffel Tower (Tour Eiffel)
Princess Diana (Unofficial) Memorial
Napoleon's Tomb
Musée de l'Armée (Army Museum)
American Cathedral in Paris
Musée des Égouts de Paris (Sewers of Paris)
National Museum of Asian Art Guimet
Musée Rodin
Fat Tire Bike Tours

Street Market: Rue Cler
Neighborhood: Rue Cler
Restaurants: Café Constant, Les Cocottes
Hotels: Hôtel du Champ de Mars, Hôtel de Varenne, Hôtel Muguet,

Near the Marais

Musée des Arts et Metiers
Place de la Bastille
Musée Carnavalet
Musée Picasso
Centre Pompidou – Musée National d'Art Moderne
Place des Vosges

Street Market: Marché Montorgueil
Restaurants: Chez Jenny, Bofinger, L'As du Fallafel
Hotels: Hôtel Sévigné, Hôtel de Nice

Near Montmartre

Sácre-Cœur
Place du Tertre
Moulin Rouge

Hotel: Hôtel Eldorado

Cruises, Walks, Tours
Bateaux Les Vedettes du Pont-Neuf
Bateaux Mouches
Canal Saint Martin-Canauxrama
Père Lachaise Cemetery (Cimetière du Père-Lachaise)
Fat Tire Bike Tours
Hop-On Hop-Off Bus (Paris l'Open Tour)

Meet Up With Other Travelers
American Cathedral in Paris
Shakespeare & Company
Jim Haynes Dinner
Fat Tire Bike Tours
HOHO Bus
L'Atelier des Chefs Cooking Class

Best Street Food
L'As du Fallafel
Berthillon
Pâtisserie Viennoise
Any crepe stand
Sandwich shops, especially those near Odeon métro
   station
Candy stand near Odeon métro station
Vin chaud (hot mulled wine) available from crepe
   stands in cold weather

Traveler Friendly Restaurants
Café Constant
Les Cocottes
Chartier
A La Petite Chaise

Le Coupe Chou
1728
Léon de Bruxelles
Au Beaujolais
Starbucks
Any Wine Bar

NOTES